VISIT THE CITY

Make the most of your time

BKB Verlag

Legend:

- ◆ opening times or departure times
- ▲ public transport stop
- ➤ see page

© BKB Verlag GmbH
All rights reserved
5/18

Editor:
Dr. Brigitte Hintzen-Bohlen

Design:
Andreas Ossig,
BKB Verlag GmbH

Translation:
Smith Translations, Hildesheim
John Sykes

Printed by:
Brandt GmbH, Bonn

ISBN 978-940914-62-0

All entries and information in this
guide have been conscientiously
researched and carefully checked.
However, it is not always possible
to rule out errors completely. We
are therefore happy to receive
suggestions for corrections and
improvements.

BKB Verlag GmbH
Auerstrasse 4
D-50733 Köln
Telephone +49 (0)221/9521460
Telefax   +49 (0)221/5626446
www.bkb-verlag.de
mail@bkb-verlag.de

Welcome to Essen ...

Winding towers and blast furnaces are things of the past – the skyline of the former coal and steel city is today dominated by office towers and glass facades. The imposing cityscape silhouette reflects Essen's significance as the business centre of the Ruhr Metropolitan Region, which is one of Europe's largest conurbations alongside London and Paris. The city is not just the region's most important service centre with outstanding competence in a host of different fields, it is also headquarters for five of the 50 most high-selling German companies.

The departure from coal and steel was accompanied by the drive towards becoming one of the most diverse and densest cultural landscapes. What used to be boiler houses and machine halls became cultural hotspots and a comparable wealth of different theatres, musical performances, museums, design and architectural achievement can be found nowhere else in Europe. The intensity of this renaissance could be seen in the region's appointment– spearheaded by Essen – to become the European Capital of Culture in 2010.

With its history spanning near 1,200 years, Essen can boast not only lovely areas and fascinating nooks and crannies, but also outstanding examples of urban culture: the cathedral and its valuable treasure, the Zollverein colliery and coking plant since 2001 – part of the World Cultural Heritage, and the Margarethenhöhe housing estate, which still conveys today a rare authentic picture of the garden city movement from the beginning of the 20th century. In the old colliery suburbs in the north of the city or in the idyllic, almost village-like settlements nestling in the green south, in the expansive green areas of the numerous local recreation sites or in its bustling centre, Essen presents itself as a captivating city that offers a host of unexpected discoveries, stimulating experiences, and lasting impressions.

About Essen

● Essen is at the centre of the RUHR METROPOLIS, the third-largest conurbation in Europe after London and Paris with a population of 5.1 million.

● In 2006 a seven-person European Union jury chose Essen, representing the whole of the Ruhr region, to be EUROPEAN CAPITAL OF CULTURE 2010.

● The global company THYSSEN-KRUPP was founded in Essen in 1811. It starts its business with only seven employees.

● The REGIONALVERBAND RUHR (regional association) has had its headquarters in Essen since it was founded in 1920. The oldest regional association in Germany, it is the umbrella organisation for the communes, consisting of four large cities and four counties.

● Since 1927 Limbacher Strasse has been closed to cars. This made it Germany's FIRST PEDESTRIAN ZONE.

● In 1934 the ESSEN MUNICIPAL PORT went into operation, the newest harbour on the Rhine-Herne Canal. Approximately one million tons of ship's cargo are loaded or unloaded here.

● Since 1958 Essen has been the seat of the BISHOPRIC OF ESSEN, a diocese that covers much of the Ruhr district and extends into the rural Sauerland region.

● The closure of the ZOLLVEREIN COKE PLANT in 1993 brought the mining history of Essen to an end.

● The trade fair grounds in Essen are the venue for the WORLD FAIR for equestrian sport, Equitana. A further popular fair is Techno-Classica, the world's biggest for veteran and vintage cars.

● On high ground called the Schurenbachhalde, an Essen landmark in the district of Altenessen, rises the SLAB FOR THE RUHR REGION.

The sculptor Richard Serra placed his 15-metre-high slab of rolled steel on this convex plateau without vegetation.

● Unlike other German cities, Essen has no Golden Book for visiting VIPs to sign, but since 1933 it has had a STEEL BOOK. The mayor at that time, Theodor Reismann-Grone, explained the name by noting that the city of Essen owed its rise to the steel industry.

● With more than 700 green spaces, some 400 playgrounds and several parks in the different parts of the city, Essen is the GREENEST CITY IN NORTH RHINE-WEST-PHALIA and the third-greenest in Germany. Part of this consists of parks and gardens that Krupp laid out in its company residential estates for the recreation of workers during the age of industrialisation.

1

8am	
9am	
10am	**Check-in at hotel**
11am	
noon	
1pm	**Meeting**

Along and alongside the culture trail
The city centre ➤ p. 10

Powerful women and unknown treasures
The cathedral ➤ p. 16

2pm	
3pm	
4pm	
5pm	
6pm	
7pm	
8pm	**Dining out** ➤ p. 44
9pm	

2

8am	
9am	**Meeting**
10am	**Missionaries and entrepreneurs** Witnesses in stone ➤ p. 22
11am	
noon	
1pm	**Dining out** ➤ p. 42
2pm	**Meeting** — **Strolling, shopping and looking around** Shopping to your heart's content ➤ p. 26
3pm	
4pm	
5pm	
6pm	
7pm	**Happy hour** ➤ p. 48
8pm	**Theatre, concert, cinema** ➤ p. 52
9pm	

3

METROPOLENSHOPPING
www.limbecker-platz.de

am

am Meeting

am | **Views, perspectives, presentations**
Museum Folkwang
➤ p. 30

am

oon

1pm Dining out
➤ p. 42

2pm

3pm The Zollverein colliery
Part of the UNESCO World Cultural Heritage
4pm ➤ p. 32

5pm

6pm Check out and depart

7pm

8pm

9pm

Services

Business trip   Short break

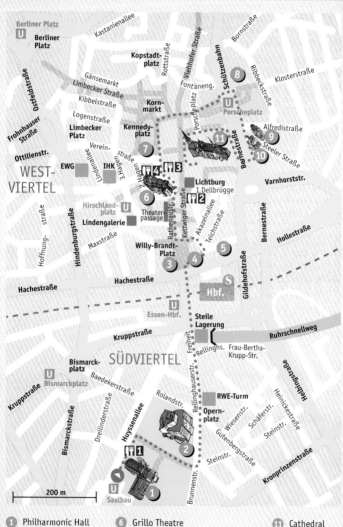

1. Philharmonic Hall
2. Aalto Theatre
3. Central Post Office
4. Hotel Handelshof
5. Haus der Technik
6. Grillo Theatre
7. Europahaus
8. Town Hall
9. Old Synagogue
10. Old Catholic Peace Church
11. Cathedral

1 Bar im Park
2 Café Solo
3 Live
4 Café Central

8am

9am

10am **Check in at hotel**

11am

noon

1pm **Meeting**

Along and alongside the culture trail –
The city centre

2pm

3pm

4pm

5pm **Powerful women and unknown treasures –**

6pm

7pm

8pm

9pm

3 Days in

The city centre
Along and alongside the culture trail

A cathedral, architecture from the Golden Twenties and skyscrapers housing corporate HQs – a stroll through downtown Essen takes you through more than 1,150 years of urban history.

Skyline
More than any other German city, the skyline of modern company headquarters reflects the economic muscle of this business location. With names like RWE AG, ThyssenKrupp AG, Aldi Nord, HOCHTIEF AG, Schenker AG, Evonik Industries AG, six of the 100 most high-selling German companies in terms of turnover have their headquarters in Essen and have made the city one of the leading decision-making centres in German business.

Saalbau
(Philharmonic Concert Hall)
KulturLinie 107

Huyssenallee 53
▲ *Philharmonie/Saalbau*
www.philharmonie-essen.de

The starting point for a city centre excursion is the Stadtgarten (City Garden) with its many sculptures, where you can view the work of artists like Ulrich Rückriem or Wilhelm Nida-Rümelin. Embedded in the green meadows to the south of the centre, a remarkable cultural ensemble has been created with the Philharmonic Concert Hall and the Opera House.

The Concert Hall with its distinctive green copper roof can already look back on a long tradition: a concert hall was opened here as early as 1864 – at that time built of wood. In the new stone building, Gustav Mahler conducted the first performance of his 6th Symphony in 1906. Following

Culture Trail
When you come across blue illuminated stones embedded in the pavement, you're following the tracks of the Culture Trail. It links places of art and culture, architecture and sculptures, and leads about four kilometres from the Museum Folkwang to the "Lichtfinger" installation at the Steag chimneys on the northern border of the city centre.

www.kulturpfadfest-essen.de

its recent con-version, the Philharmonic KulturLinie 107 is regarded as one of the best in Europe thanks to its modern equipment and outstanding acoustics.

Aalto Theatre (Opera House)
Opernplatz 10
▲ *Hauptbahnhof*
www.aalto-musiktheater.de

An architectural highlight of international repute is just a bit further on: Alvar Aalto's theatre in bright granite. The design concept from the noted Finnish architect had already won the architectural competition for a music theatre

»Have a break«
At **Bar im Park** you have a wonderful view of the Stadtgarten park from the terrace while enjoying culinary treats.
Sheraton Essen Hotel, Huyssenallee 55,
◆ *Mon-Fri 10-1am, Sat-Sun 11am-midnight*

in Essen in 1954. He did not live to see its realisation, however, because 30 years went by before the grand opening.

The harmoniously rolling, asymmetrical exterior remains fascinating to this day. Vaguely reminiscent of a tree stump, it reflects Aalto's aesthetic conception of a "humane architecture". In his view, nature provides the model for an edifice, which should blend into the landscape. These gentle contours are continued inside the building down to the smallest detail. You should take in a performance alone to experience the auditorium, which is designed in the Finnish national colours blue and white: it is laid out like an ancient amphitheatre with ascending, semicircular rows of seats. A special kind of musical adventure!

until 2.30pm

KulturLinie 107

Power-Tower ...
... is the popular name for the tallest office building in the Ruhr district, a 162-metre-high skyscraper built by the Düsseldorf-based architect Christoph Ingenhoven. This is the home of the RWE energy group, which has created in its tower a symbol of the region's fitness to meet future challenges. Like no other building, the Power Tower is an emblem of Essen as the city of company headquarters and Europe's "energy capital". The view over the Ruhr Metropolitan Region from the platform 120 metres above ground level is spectacularly unique.

Opernplatz 1
Tel. 0800/0703700
www.rwe.com
▲ *Hauptbahnhof*

Conducted tours:
3rd Sat each month
(March-Oct)
10am-3pm
on the hour

from 2.30pm

KulturLinie 107

Grillo Theatre
Theaterplatz 11
▲ *Hirschlandplatz*
*www.schauspiel-
essen.de*

The city of Essen can boast one of the oldest theatres in the Ruhr region: the neo-Classicistic building was a present from the industrialist Friedrich Grillo that was realised by his widow in 1892. What is today the City Theatre keeps alive the memory of the son of a

merchant family in Essen who had a decisive influence on the economic and structural development of the Ruhr region through his business empire.

"Steile Lagerung" monument

In the south section of the city centre behind the rail station the cityscape is marked by modern high-rise tower blocks: major companies like RWE, Hochtief or Evonik are headquartered here. A bronze symbol of the structural change undergone in the region is the *"Steile Lagerung"* ("Steep Bearing") monument sculpted by Max Kratz (1989) in front of the Evonik HQ. It honours the miners and their arduous work underground that shaped the city's image for centuries. It was only with the closure of the Zollverein colliery in 1986 that this tradition came to a final end.

Office buildings

The walk continues to the railway station, where early Modernist commercial and office buildings on Bahnhofsvorplatz show that Essen was already a flourishing city with a metropolitan character in the early 20th century. It's not far from the gigantic, expressionist brick complex on the Hachestrasse (1924 – 1933), the *central post* office, to the protected group of buildings containing the Hotel Mövenpick (Am Hauptbahnhof 2). This is where the parents of the famous thespian Heinz Rühmann opened the *Hotel Handelshof* within the 6-storey hotel and commercial building in 1913.

The striking brick construction opposite the station with the arcade walkway along the Hollestrasse served as the seat of the stock exchange after it was completed in 1925 by Edmund Körner, the architect of the Essen synagogue. Nowadays, the office and commercial building is a well-equipped convention centre, where the *Haus der Technik*, or HDT for short, stages over 1,500 events each year (Hollestrasse 1).

KulturLinie 107

The U-shaped complex on the Kennedy Square hales from a later era: it was erected in 1952 under the name "Amerikahaus" as a symbol of German-American understanding. For more than 10 years the building has now been known in Essen as the *Europahaus*: it is home to Stratmann's Theatre, where the doctor and political satirist Ludger Stratmann, or others, take the stage (➤ p. 54).

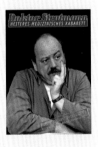

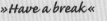

»Have a break« **M2**

Near Lichtburg you'll always find a nice place in the **Café Solo**, where you can watch the comings and goings on Essen´s shoping mile.
Kettwiger Strasse 36,
◆ *Mon-Sat from 8.30am,*
Sun from 9am

KulturLinie 107

The Lichtburg
*Kettwiger Strasse 36
(city centre)
Tickets 0201/231023
Programme info
0201/231024*
▲ *Hirschlandplatz*
*www.lichtburg-
essen.de*

The cinema situated in the heart of Essen remains a legend in its own right! Opened in 1928 as Germany's largest film palace with 1,250 seats, it has survived bombing raids, economic crises and the competition from its multiplex rivals. After the post-war reconstruction of Germany, the elegant movie theatre grew into Germany's main venue for film premieres in the 1950s and 1960s: alongside first nights, gala presentations and world premieres, its stage also hosted theatrical, satirical and concert performances. Since its glamorous reopening in 2003, the cinema has taken up its former function once again.

13

The future is on the way

On a site of some 230 hectares west of the inner city, the former Krupp factory for cast steel where Alfred Krupp once produced his famous wheels, a major and spectacular urban project to create residential, commercial and leisure space is

going ahead. The heart of the so-called Krupp-gürtel (Krupp belt) is the ThyssenKrupp Quartier, headquarters of the company with places of work for 2,000 employees. Access to the new quarter will be provided by the Berthold-Beitz-Boulevard, and its green lung will be the Krupp-Park with five hills, a lake fed by the rainwater of the surroundings, and areas of woodland and grass.

www.thyssenkrupp.com/quartier

Town Hall
Porscheplatz
▲ *Porscheplatz*
◆ *Mon, Tue & Thu 7am-4pm, Wed 7am-3.30pm, Fri 7am-3pm*

Guided Tours: 0201/8815304

Sandstone figures from the previous building representing the patrons of Essen, Saint Cosmas and Saint Damian, stand in the lobby of Essen's city hall, one of the tallest city halls in Europe with a height of 106 metres. Visitors who take a tour of the building can see from the upper storeys the transformation of Essen that has taken in recent years. Where once stood blast furnaces and smoking chimneys, you now see a modern skyline.

Old Synagogue   `KulturLinie 107`
Steeler Strasse 29
▲ *Porscheplatz*
◆ *Tue-Sun 10am-6pm*
www.alte-synagoge.essen.de

One of Germany's largest and finest synagogues, built between 1911 and 1913, it was used for a long time as a forum for documentation and a place of memorial and encounters. Since its renovation this house of Jewish culture informs visitors about the history of the Jewish community in Essen, about Jewish religion and traditions, and is a place to encounter Jewish culture and the Jewish way of life.

Jahrhundertbrunnen (Century Fountain)
Corner of Bernestrasse/Steeler Strasse

"Spry to work – happy at rest" can be read in German on the fountain at the corner and a smith symbolises the city's upswing thanks to the coal and steel industry. The shell limestone fountain was created in 1907 to mark the centenary of Essen's membership in the Prussian state.

Old Catholic Peace Church (Friedenskirche)

`KulturLinie 107`

Bernestrasse 1
◆ *Wed 3-5pm + by appointment through the rectory, Tel. 0201/223763 or 9587280*

The Old Catholic Peace Church houses a real treasure: inside the unpretentious building from 1916 with its imposing tower, art nouveau paintings from the Dutch artist Jan Thorn Prikker (1868–1932) have survived in the apse. The ornamental gold mosaic was funded through a donation from the Krupp family of industrialists. The work gives an impression of the former glory of this Jugendstil church, whose ceiling frescoes were destroyed by Second World War bombing raids.

The restored ceiling of the galleries also hints at the erstwhile splendour: the frescoes are a stylised representation of a lace fabric that is also the night sky.

Gustav Heinemann
The reconstruction of Essen is inseparable from the figure of Gustav Heinemann (1899–1976), who became the city's Chief Mayor in 1946. He had lived and worked in Essen since the 1920s and his political career began after the war: Minister of Justice in North-Rhine Westphalia, Federal Minister of the Interior in Adenauer's first cabinet (which the committed pacifist left in protest against the rearmament in 1950), Federal Minister of Justice, and finally German Federal President from 1969–1974. His name remains linked with a commitment to civil and human rights.

»*Have a break*« `M3`
Bistro **Fun Factory** at the VHS education college is a good place to take a break with fresh wraps, crepes and pastries
Burgplatz 1, ◆ *Mon-Fri 9am-10pm, Sat 10am-6pm*

Powerful women and unknown treasures

The cathedral KulturLinie 107

Many are surprised to hear Essen has a cathedral. That it also houses art treasures of world repute is hardly known at all. Surrounded by modern-style buildings, the former collegiate church draws its visitors into the city's medieval past.

The cathedral
Burgplatz 2 (City)
▲ *Porscheplatz*
◆ *Mon, Fri 10am-6.30pm, Tue-Thu 6.30am-6.30pm, Sat-Sun 9am-7.30pm*
www.dom-essen.de

Building chronicle
In 852 Altfrid, Bishop of Hildesheim, founded a college of canonesses and laid the foundation stone for its church. It was consecrated in 870 and Altfrid was buried there four years later. The cathedral was destroyed by fire many times: the western section dates back to a new building erected by the abbess Mathilde, whereas the nave and choir were rebuilt in the Gothic style in 1275. In 1803, when religious houses were dissolved, it became the parish church of St John the Baptist, and in 1958 was officially declared the cathedral of the Ruhr diocese.

What did the rich noble families do with their unmarried daughters and widows in the Middle Ages? They were banished into a ladies' convent, where they had to swear an oath of celibacy but could marry anytime if they relinquished their maintenance. Essen's cathedral building from 852 has its roots in such as "care facility". Under the auspices of various abbesses from the Ottonian imperial dynasty, the convent increasingly gained power and influence and even gained territorial sovereignty in the 13th century.

It is then only natural that these abbesses have placed their stamp on the architecture and interior of the collegiate church: the structural highlight of the three-nave hall church is the Romanesque West section built under Abbess Theophanu (1039–1058), granddaughter of Emperor Otto II.

With its three octagonal towers, the hexa-gonal layout of the ground plan and the artistic wall arrangement, the West section is reminiscent of the Palatine Chapel built in Aachen at the palace of Charlemagne, the first "Roman" emperor since antiquity. With such a model the abbess wanted to symbolically place her regency in that illustrious tradition.

The cathedral owes several art treasures of worldwide significance to Abbess Mathilde II (971–1011), a granddaughter of Emperor Otto the Great. She gave Essen "its treasure", as the *Golden Madonna* is popularly called: the sculpture in the left side-chapel is 70 centimetres tall and the oldest known three--dimensional depiction of the Virgin Mary in the world. It is one of the most famous masterpieces from the Ottonian period. The figure was cut from lime-tree wood, covered with gold foil and decorated with precious stones.

Mathilde also donated a seven-armed candelabrum to the collegiate church, which now stands in the basement of the West section. The two-metre-high bronze candelabrum is a replica of the cult object housed in the Temple of Solomon and is the oldest surviving example of its kind. It was joined together out of almost 50 individual parts.

Visitors can pay their respects to the church's founder: the remains of St. Altfrid rest in a Gothic table tomb in the crypt.

City patrons Cosmas and Damian
Stone figures on the choir pillars such as the sword on the city arms commemorate the two twin brothers from Arabia: they practised as doctors and report-edly converted many people to Christian-ity through their free treatment of the ill. During the persecution of Christians under the Roman Emperor Dio-cletian, they were ar-rested and wondrously rescued several times before they were finally beheaded. After Altfrid passed their relics on to the convent, they became its patrons and later the patron saints of the entire city.

3 **Days in**

IBA or ...
a region changes its look. The *International Building Exhibition (IBA) Emscher Park* (1989–1999) produced stimuli that influenced the self-conception of an entire region. With the modernisation of old factory architecture, the renaturalisation of brownfield sites and the redevelopment of industrial monuments like the Zollverein colliery, the IBA has elaborated planning approaches that have become international models.

St. John's Church of Worship

There's something particularly interesting to see to the left of the atrium: the four surviving altar panels that Bartholomaeus Bruyn painted in the early 16th century for the collegiate church stand in the three-nave Gothic hall church. The oldest known depiction of the city panorama of Essen can be seen in the background of the "Deposition from the Cross"!

One may indeed wonder why there are two churches lying next to each other here. In the Middle Ages it was quite usual to link a main and a succursal church by means of an atrium. This subsidiary church was originally a baptistery and therefore dedicated to St. John the Baptist before it was overbuilt in the 15th century. On account of the limited space available at the time, the builders chose the unusual square layout with straight choir at the end.

Cathedral treasury

Burgplatz 2

KulturLinie 107

♦ *Tue-Sat 10am-5pm, Sun 11.30am-5pm*
Guided tours: Tel. 0201/2204206
www.domschatz-essen.de

Signaltafel Schacht 8
Bühne

A visit to the treasury makes it clear just how much the city profited from the reign of the abbesses. These women controlled the fate of the convent and city for almost 1,000 years and enriched the church treasury with valuable works of art. A unique collection of outstanding artworks of ottonian and salian can be admired here today.

Looking at the small enamel plate at the foot of the collection's most famous piece, one can discover the benefactors: it was Duke Otto of Bavaria and Schwabia who handed over the Procession Crucifix to his sister Mathilde, the abbess of the Essen cloister (971–1011). Look at the figure of Christ on the Otto-Mathilde Crucifix: it is not superimposed but has been pushed out of the gold plating of the cross and then framed by pearly, jewels and filigree decoration.

"Fellow Franz"

... was the nickname given to the founding bishop of the Ruhr Diocese, Franz Hengsbach (1910–1991), throughout the coalfields. He had a firm place in people's hearts even after he died. After he took office in 1958, he took continuous care of his fold: he not only gave them hope and assurance when the collieries began to close and the steel crisis loomed, but also gave them new perspectives. His commitment led to the Ruhr Region Initiative Group with leading representatives from business and industry to overcome the structural crisis.

3 years old and already a king? Otto II made it possible: in 983 he made his three-year-old son, the later Otto III, co-regent of the Holy Roman Empire. If the babe really wore the Children's Crown made of gold plate and decorated with pearls and jewels at his inauguration on Christmas Day, however, is uncertain.

The golden book cover of the Theophanu Gospel from the first half of the 11th century shows how sumptuously manuscripts were preserved during the Middle Ages: an ivory panel in the centre depicts scenes from the birth, crucifixion and ascension of Christ.

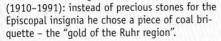

The fact that the scale was somewhat more modest in the 20th century is evidenced by the Bishop's Ring from Cardinal Franz Hengsbach (1910–1991): instead of precious stones for the Episcopal insignia he chose a piece of coal briquette – the "gold of the Ruhr region".

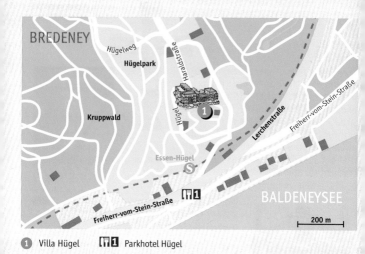

1 Villa Hügel    1 Parkhotel Hügel

2 St. Ludgerus   3 St. Lucius   2 Abraham Konditorei & Café Werntges

am

am **Meeting**

am **Missionaries and entrepreneurs –
Witnesses in stone**

1pm **Dining out**. . . . . ➤ p. 42

2pm **Meeting** **Strolling, shopping and
looking around**

3pm

4pm

5pm

6pm

7pm **Happy hour** . . . . ➤ p. 48

8pm **Theatre, concert, cinema** . . . . ➤ p. 52

9pm

from 10am

Witnesses in stone
Missionaries and entrepreneurs

Entrepreneur and benefactor ...
was the man who created a symbol of his power in the form of the Villa Hügel. Alfred Krupp took over the debt-ridden cast steel factory at the under age of 14 after his father died and made it world-famous. Seamless railway tyres were his big sellers, steam hammers and the Bessemer process were his innovative production techniques.

But he also took great care of his employees: he built them houses, introduced health insurance, and granted longstanding Krupp workers a pension. This established a tradition of philanthropy that flourishes in Essen to this day: with about 200 charitable foundations, it is one of Germany's leading cities in this field.

This journey takes us from the imposing residence of the family that gave Essen its name "Kruppstadt" to the last Romanesque church on the Rhine and Ruhr.

Villa Hügel   `KulturLinie 107`
Hügel 15 (Bredeney)
▲ *Essen-Hügel*
◆ *Tue-Sun 10am-6pm (villa), daily 8am-8pm (park)*
Tel. 0201/616290
www.villahuegel.de

Who hasn't dreamed of living in a residence like this? 629 rooms covering 8,100 square metres, a ballroom almost as large as that in Berlin's imperial palace, an expansive 28-hectare park complete with botanical gardens – and all that embedded in an attractive elevated landscape above Lake Baldeney. The building erected by Alfred Krupp in 1873 according to his own plans to be his family's domicile and the representative address of his company is more like a palace than a villa.

Villa Hügel is always worth a visit, even when none of the high-calibre art exhibitions are currently running. The villa has been open to the public since 1954, which enables us to view the historic rooms, inform ourselves about company and family history, or just simply saunter through the impressive park grounds.

Entering the official salons and parlours on the ground floor of the Great House, what used to be the main residence, one can easily sense what took place here earlier behind the polished Classicistic stone facades

of this immense estate. Emperors, kings and industrialists were guests here since the villa also served for official receptions given by the global Krupp empire. There were times when almost 650 people worked within its grounds and a special infrastructure comprising gas and electricity works, rail station, manor business and telecommunication system was developed and purpose-built to support the enterprise.

The rooms have been preserved in their 1915 condition, with luxurious wooden panelling, bulky furniture and copious works of art. The collection of Flemish tapestries dating from 1500 to 1760 is unique and the technical standard in the residence is truly impressive: the owner laid great store by modern technology in its construction.

The Ruhr Culture Foundation resides in the Great House at the moment. The foundation stages the major, international art exhibitions.

The permanent exhibitions are housed in the former guesthouse, the Small House. The park contains trees that are older than the entire estate. Alfred planted fully-grown trees because he wanted to be able to enjoy his park during his own lifetime.

Housing welfare in the 20th century: Margarethenhöhe

▲ *Halbe Höhe*
Show house:
Am Brückenkopf/
Ecke Steile Strasse
For info call
0201/24681444
www.ruhrmuseum.de

As Margarethe, the widow of Friedrich Alfred Krupp, donated grounds to the west of Rüttenscheid and the necessary building capital to an endowment for housing welfare purposes, the foundation was laid for one of the loveliest garden suburbs. A purpose-built yet comfortable housing estate was created for several thousand inhabitants over the next 20 years according to the plans of the architect Georg Metzendorf. The picturesque ensemble is dominated by gables, arcades, oriels and shutters. Despite a variety of architectural styles it still conveys the impression of a self-contained entity.

»Have a break« 🛏1
For lunch you can enjoy regional cuisine in what was once the canteen of Villa Hügel, in the restaurant of **Parkhaus Hügel**, with a view of the Baldeneysee.
Freiherr-von-Stein-Strasse 209 ♦ Mon-Fri from 2.30pm, Sat-Sun from 11.30am

until 11.30am

from 11.30am

Folkwang University of the Arts

The cultural landmark of the city is the world-famous Folkwang University of the Arts. The college of Music, Theatre and Dance, Design and Academic Studies continues the traditional Folkwang idea (➤ p. 30) of an interdisciplinary collaboration between different artistic directions. The college has brought forth a number

of famous dancers, directors, musicians and actors, including Pina Bausch and Armin Rohde. Around 1,600 students visit the college, whose main location is situated in the Baroque building of the historic Werden Abbey.

Klemensborn 39
▲ *Essener Markt*
www.folkwang-uni.de

Essen-Werden
▲ *Essen-Werden, Werdener Markt*

The beginnings of the Werden district are closely connected with the missionary Liudger. He founded a Benedictine monastery above the Ruhr valley around 800 AD; the successor buildings still dominate the cityscape. Thanks to the location's good accessibility, a flourishing locality rapidly grew up around the cloister, which was given its town charter in 1317. Today, the district has a charming Old Town with slate-covered half-timbered houses.

St. Ludgerus
Brückstrasse 54
◆ *9am-6pm, treasury: Tue-Sun 10am-noon, 3pm-5pm, www.st-ludgerus-werden.de, www.schatzkammer-werden.de*

As the last Romanesque church in the Rhine-land, Werden abbey has found its place in the history books. At the time the construction of the cathedral began, a three-nave arcade basilica was built here in late Romanesque style. It has been preserved in its original state except for the Baroque intersection tower that was added later.

The new construction, which became necessary after the fire of 1256 and also included older parts like the 10th century western section and the outside crypt, was consecrated in 1275 by Albertus Magnus.

Anyone wishing to know more about the legend surrounding the foundation of Werden should cast a glance at the Baroque high altar. The central depiction relates the "Tree Wonder":

Liudger had determined a place under a tree as his final resting-place, which became an attraction for many pilgrims as the *locus arboris*. When the painting is raised, a statue of the cloister founder appears that is being lifted up to heaven by angels.

The *treasury* is also well worth a visit: alongside a pyxis from late antiquity, which presumably served as container for altar bread or relics, there is also a Franconian relic case from the 8th century to admire. Whether the oak case with carved ivory panels was indeed the portable altar of Saint Liudger is not known.

St. Luzius
Luziusstrasse
◆ On request

Since the number of Christians in Werden constantly increased, the abbey established a subsidiary church a few hundred metres away in 995, which was extended into a three-nave basilica in the 11th century. It is regarded as the oldest existing parish church north of the Alps and houses high-quality stonemasonry and the remains of murals depicting saints and abbots.

Essen-Kettwig
The idyllic Kettwig district situated in attractive countryside in the southernmost bend of the River Ruhr is well worth a detour: in the picturesque Old Town the evangelical market church overlooks the numerous half-timbered houses. Many cafes and taverns in the area tempt visitors to stop and linger a while. The Ruhr panorama is dominated by the Scheidt cloth factory, the largest company in the former cloth-making town that, in contrast to the surrounding communities, possessed hardly any coal or mineral resources.

»Have a break« [m]2
During the summer, a touch of Italian flair can almost be felt in the idyllic Grafenstrasse. It's worth stopping off for coffee and cakes in the **Abraham Konditorei & Café Werntges.**
Grafenstr. 36-38, ◆ *Mon-Fri 8.30am-6.30pm, Sat 9.30am-6.30pm, Sun 10am-6.30pm*

until 1pm

from 2pm

Strolling, shopping and looking around –
Shopping to your heart's content

Window of culture
If you would like information about the variety of cultural life in Essen, take a walk to the Generationen-KultHaus. Thanks to an initiative of the city cultural office and Lokalfieber Essen City-Nord, the new Culture Window is presented there. Here every month cultural facilities and artists can display their work.

Viehofer Strasse 31
♦ *Starts on the 1st Wednesday of the month*

Around Kettwiger Strasse, on Limbecker Platz or the Rü, shopping in Essen is a pleasure in many different places.

When you leave the main railway station, a slogan in lights above the Handelshof catches the eye: "Essen – Die Einkaufsstadt" (shopping city). The sign is old, but its message is still modern. *Kettwiger Strasse*, an extensive pedestrian precinct, starts here with the department store Galeria Kaufhof. All the way to the Viehofer Platz, various boutiques, emporia, branches of international store chains and long-established retailers offer a host of wares to browse and buy. There's a lot going on here at all times of the day and year.

Sometime at the top of the hour, one has to take up position outside the jewellers Deiter (Kettwiger Strasse 22): for that is when the miner on the bell tower strikes out the time. The *Glockenspiel* (or carillon), whose 26 bells play various tunes throughout the day from 9 to 7, dates from 1928.

At the Porsche-platz a visit to the *Rathaus Galerie* is well worthwhile: you can wander through 80 shops here – and not just if the weather's bad. Other arcades are attractive places for window shopping:

the *Theaterpassage*, a protected monument dating from the 1920s, has high-quality goods, and the *Lindengalerie* in the Deutschlandhaus opposite is smaller ...

The central office of the *Sparkasse Essen* (III. Hagen 43) is also worth looking at. The savings bank acts as patron for Essen's cultural scene and stages interesting in-house exhibitions.

The area around *Limbecker Strasse* attracts younger shoppers, who find fashion items in chic boutiques, flagship stores and branches of the well-known chains. A new retail highlight is on *Limbecker Platz*. Here one of the largest German shopping centres of the

The West End
A new district called the weststadt has emerged where the Krupp factory grounds once sprawled. The area is seen as a prime example of the successful fusion of monument conservation and urban development. The entrance area has been preserved from the original industrial premises: the VIII Mechanical Workshop from the turn of the last century has become a venue for musicals, the Colosseum theatre Essen (➤ p. 52), and the building opposite is used by IKEA as a multi-storey car park. The former repair hall "*west*stadtHalle" has been taken over by the Folkwang School of Music.The Cinemaxx cinema complex (➤ p. 55) has been recently erected. It's probably clear that there's a lot going down during the evenings.

»Have a break« 🎬4
For those seeking respite from the bustle of the shopping area, **Coffee Pirates in Rüttenscheid** is just the right place.
Rüttenscheiderstr. 218
◆ Tue-Sat 9am-6pm,
Sun 10am-6pm

inner city has an area of over 70,000 square metres with 200 shops for bargain hunters and all those who want to take a break in a trendy location.

Things are a little quieter on the *Rü*, as the locals fondly call Rüttenscheider Strasse. Whether you are looking for fine foods or designer furniture, with its boutiques, small independent stores, restaurants and cafés is one of the most popular and entertaining streets in the city for shopping and strolling.

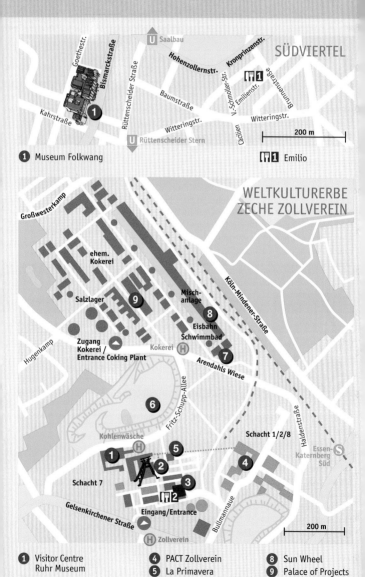

SÜDVIERTEL

Goethestr.
Bismarckstraße
Kahrstraße
U Saalbau
Hohenzollernstr.
Rüttenscheider Straße
Baumstraße
Kronprinzenstr.
V.-Schmoller-Str.
Emilienstr.
Brunnenstraße
Witteringstr.
Cäcilien
Witteringstr.
U Rüttenscheider Stern

200 m

1 Museum Folkwang

🏛1 Emilio

WELTKULTURERBE ZECHE ZOLLVEREIN

Großwesterkamp
ehem. Kokerei
Salzlager
Zugang Kokerei / Entrance Coking Plant
Hugenkamp
Mischanlage
Köln-Mindener-Straße
Eisbahn Schwimmbad
Kokerei (H)
Arendahls Wiese
Kohlenwäsche (H)
Fritz-Schupp-Allee
Schacht 1/2/8
Haldenstraße
Essen-Katernberg Süd (S)
Schacht 7
🏛2
Eingang/Entrance
Gelsenkirchener Straße
Bullmannaue
(H) Zollverein

200 m

1. Visitor Centre Ruhr Museum
2. Winding Tower
3. Red Dot Design Museum
4. PACT Zollverein
5. La Primavera
6. Sculpture Forest
7. Coking Plant
8. Sun Wheel
9. Palace of Projects

🏛2 Casino Zollverein

8am

9am **Meeting**

10am **Views, perspectives, presentations**
Museum Folkwang Essen ..... ➤ p. 30

11am

noon

1pm **Dining out** .... ➤ p. 42

2pm

3pm **Part of the UNESCO World Cultural Heritage –
The Zollverein colliery**

4pm Zollverein colliery – Shaft XII and coking plant ...... ➤ p. 32

5pm

6pm **Check-out and depart**

7pm

8pm

9pm

Views, perspectives, presentations
Museum Folkwang

The forerunners of modern art and the Expressionists, American Color Field painting and the German Informel movement, photography, graphic art, posters and applied arts – all of this can be admired in the Museum Folkwang, Europe's first museum for contemporary art.

Museum Folkwang   `KulturLinie 107`
Bismarckstr. 60, (South Quarter)
▲ *Rüttenscheider Stern*
♦ *Tue-Wed, Sat-Sun 10am-6pm, Thu-Fri 10am-8pm*
Tel. 0201/8845444
www.museum-folkwang.de

Folkwang ...
... comes from the collection of Norse mythic verse known as the "Edda". When the art collector and patron Karl Ernst Osthaus (1874–1921) established a museum in Hagen in 1902, he chose the name of the hall of Freya, the Germanic goddess of love and beauty. And art and beauty is what visitors were to encounter in the new museum, which was purchased when Osthaus died in 1922 and moved to Essen. The name became programmatic here: at the latest when the Folkwang College (➤ p. 24) was founded in 1927, the name stands for a synthesis of the arts and the idea of collecting all art forms under one roof.

It is remarkable for a museum to be able to claim that hardly a single prominent artist of the 19th and 20th centuries is absent from its collection. The foundations for this unique range of art were laid by the Folkwang Museum of Karl Ernst Osthaus, whose collection was united with that of the city museum of art in 1922. In the following years, under the direction of Ernst Gosebruch, the museum was able to expand its holdings by means of selected purchases, and became world famous. However, little remained after 1945, as over 1,400 works were confiscated during the Third Reich as being "degenerate", and the museum building was destroyed. Through repurchases and new acquisitions, the gaps were filled and the collection extended to include contemporary art, so that today the Museum Folkwang is regarded as one of Germany's most renowned museums of art.

SKY KIEFER KIRCHNER KIRKEBY KLEE KLEIN
CHKA KRULL KÜHN LEHMBRUCK LEIBL
LIEBERMANN LOUIS LÜPERTZ MACK MACKE
TTE MANET MANRAY MAREES MATISSE
L MINNE MIRÓ MODEL MODERSOHN-BECKER
Y-NAGY MONDRIAN MONET MUELLER MUNCH
EWMAN NOLDE PISSARRO PECHSTEIN PENCK
O PIENE POLKE POLLOCK REINHARDT REN-
TZSCH RENOIR RICHTER ROHLFS ROSSO
O ROTTMANN RUFF SALOMON SANDER
EL SCHMIDT-ROTTLUFF SCHULTZE SCHUMA-
SCHÜTTE SCULLY SHERMAN SIGNAC SMITH
GE STEICHEN STEINERT STELLA TANGUY
TOBEY TRÜBNER UECKER UMBO VLAMINCK

In time for the region's year as European Capital of Culture, a new and extended building designed by the London architect David Chipperfield is completed, thanks to the support of the Alfried Krupp von Bohlen und Halbach Foundation.

On an exhibition space totalling about 6,200 square metres, visitors are able to gain an almost complete overview of German and French painting in the 19th and 20th centuries – from German Romantic painting and French landscapes to Impressionism, Expressionism, Cubism and the Bauhaus, from the modern movement right through to contemporary art.

The *Graphic Art Collection*, which includes 12,000 items from the 19th and 20th centuries, is closely bound up with the history and conception of the collection of paintings.

A third focus is the *Photographic Collection*, which provides a comprehensive survey of photography since the 19th century.

In addition there is a collection deriving from Osthaus' bequest and displaying items of applied art from Germany, Europe and non-European countries.

The *German Poster Museum* is a further highlight. On the premises of the Museum Folkwang it exhibits its specialised collection, the world's biggest, of large-format posters from the fields of politics, commerce and culture, and thus traces the evolution of the poster from its beginnings to the present day.

Energy Trading Floor

What does it take to enable 250 traders to analyse the markets for energy all at the same time and to trade in electricity and its raw materials on European and world markets? Find out for yourself on a visit to the HQ of RWE Supply Trading. This energy trading company, part of the RWE group, is based right next to the Victoria Mathias coal mine, the historic cradle of

the major energy corporation RWE. At the heart of the complex is the trading floor, 2,900 square metres in size and 7 metres high, a room like a stock exchange and the largest of its kind in Europe.

» Have a break « M1

If you need refreshment after looking at the art, try the delicious food at **Vincent & Paul**. *(in Museum Folkwang)*
◆ Tue-Sat 11am-11pm, Sun 11am-6pm

The Zollverein colliery
Part of the UNESCO World Cultural Heritage

Shut down yet immortal

The story of the colliery began in 1847, when the businessman Franz Haniel bought the coalfield to the city's Northeast and named it after the German Customs and Trading Association, an economic alliance of German states.

Four years later, the first anthracite could be extracted and the number of workers had risen to 5,000 by the turn of the century. Following reparation demands, occupation and economic crises in the aftermath of the First World War, the construction of the highly efficient shaft system was decided upon in 1926. A coking plant was added in 1957–1961.

A world-famous double winding tower, old industrial buildings in modern dress, design, art and culture make up today's picture of the facilities that – like no other – are a symbol of the transformation of the entire Ruhr region.

Zollverein colliery Shaft XII and Zollverein coking plant

Smoking chimneys, coal dumps, winding towers, cooling towers – wherever one looks. What is so valuable about the architectural remains of this era that the UNESCO declared them to be part of the World Cultural Heritage – one or two visitors may ask themselves. And they'll be astonished …

… at the technical standard: when Zollverein colliery Shaft XII started operation sin 1932, it had been installed according to the latest mining engineer- ing standards. In terms of the quantities extracted, it remained the leader in Europe until its closure in 1986. The coking plant was also considered the most advanced of its kind on the continent for a long time.

... at the Bauhaus-architecture, which appears at once functional and aesthetic and has been worked out in its smallest details.

... at the conception of the layout: the building elements are clearly arranged according to the sequence of production and in harmony with the two main axes, the 55 metres high pithead frame and the demolished smokestack of the boiler house.

What the architects Fritz Schupp and Martin Kremmer created with this facility is an integrated work of art unsurpassed in construction and engineering terms until the decline of the coal, iron and steel industry. Today, a new chapter has started: a business, design and cultural centre is being created on the grounds of the colliery and coking plant by the world-famous architect Rem Koolhaas.

An image of this industrial monument has gone around the world and become a symbol for the new Ruhr region. It meets the eye immediately in the so-called Ehrenhof: a 55-metre-high *winding tower* that is painted rust-red.

The starting point for visits and all tours is the former coal washing plant, the largest above-ground building of Zollverein colliery, which was converted from a machine hall into a museum. A 58-metre-long, free-standing escalator goes up to the 24-metre level and leads into the *international visitor centre*, which accommodates all service functions such as the information and ticket desk, the cloakroom, café and shop.

Zollverein Shaft XII
Gelsenkirchener Strasse 181
(Katernberg)
▲ Zollverein
◆ The grounds are freely accessible.
Tel. 0201/246810
www.zollverein.de

Visitor centre Zollverein, Shaft XII (Hall 2, upper floor)
Building A 14
◆ 10am-6pm
Guided tours:
Tel. 0201/246810,
Route of Industrial Heritage:
Tel. 0201/24498932
www.route-industriekultur.de

Zollverein coking plant
Arendahls Wiese
(Katernberg)
Building C 70
▲ Altenessen Bahnhof
◆ Mon-Fri 11am-3pm,
Sat-Sun 11am-5pm
Tel. 0201/8301275

Route of Industrial Heritage

If you want to view important industrial plants, worker housing estates or museums, enjoy the view from special lookout points, or just inform yourself about the region's past, you should follow part of the Route of Industrial Heritage. The 400 kilometre long excursion takes you through 150 years of industrial culture and presents a landscape of 52 examples of the Ruhr region's industrial culture past and present. 25 thematic routes illuminating specific aspects start out from various anchor points.

Zollverein visitor centre (➤ p. 33)
www.route-industriekultur.de

At the same time it serves as the foyer for the *Ruhr Museum*, which will inaugurate its permanent exhibition here in january 2010. The museum, which incorporates the collections of the former Ruhrlandmuseum in Essen on geology, archaeology, history and photography, sees its role as the memory and shop-window of the new Ruhr metropolis, and will present the fascinating history of one of the world's greatest industrial regions. The museum tour covering three floors tells the story of the present-day Ruhr cities, the geological background, developments in pre-industrial times and the process of industrialisation in the Ruhr area.

Tel. 0201/24681444
◆ 10am-6pm
www.ruhrmuseum.de

After this the next stop is the screening plant, where normal stone and large pieces of coal were separated by hand on slowly moving conveyor belts. The rooms on the upper floor are used today for events, and on the ground floor there is an opportunity to look round shops and artists' studios.

Lovers of contemporary design are drawn above all to a building which for its architecture alone is one of the attractions of the site: since its conversion by the British architect Lord Norman Foster, the old boiler house has been home to the *red dot design museum* and the Design Centre of North-Rhine Westphalia. Visitors to what is the world's largest exhibition of its

kind can admire some 1,500 items of everyday and consumer culture from all around the world on an area of over 4,000 square metres. From wrist watches and mobile phones to kitchen appliances and cars, products which have all been winners of the red dot design award

can be discovered amongst the old industrial equipment.

Tel. 0201/3010460,
◆ *Tue-Sun 11am-6pm*
www.red-dot.de

An out-of-the-ordinary experience awaits visitors in the former ash bunker, the site of an unusual installation by the American artist Maria Nordman entitled "*La Primavera*". The way through the interior, which is closed to view from outside and

One chapter of industrial history
As Friedrich Krupp set up a factory to produce cast steel in 1811, he could hardly have imagined that he was founding a company of global dimensions. His son Alfred expanded the Krupp family business into Europe's largest industrial enterprise at the time. The three rings that make up the company logo represent his greatest invention, a seamless, forged and rolled tyre for the railways. Since the invention of the cannon tube made of cast steel in 1847, weapons production became a dominant element in company history. However, the concern took up new directions in 1945. The latest chapter began in 1999: Krupp merged with Thyssen to become ThyssenKrupp AG.

Friedrich Krupp, the founder of the steel empire

»Have a break« 🎟2
If you need a break after so much technology and design, you can choose between "miner cooking" and New World Cuisine in the former compressor hall, the **Casino Zollverein.**
Gelsenkirchener Strasse 181, Tel. 0201/830240
◆ *Tue-Fri 11.30am-3pm, 5.30pm-midnight, Sat 1pm-midnight, Sun 11.30am-midnight*

From coal to energy

A glance at Essen's skyline shows not only its transformation from a centre of coal and steel production to a services city, but also reveals the importance of Essen as Germany's leading location for the energy sector: Whether RWE, E.ON or Evonik all the big players in the energy business have their corporate headquarters here. Together with numerous small and medium-sized production and service companies, many of them highly specialised, research institutes, associations of the energy industry and trade fairs, they make the city one of the hubs of the European energy sector.

can be entered only by one person at a time, leads into a "White Cube", an empty, dimly lit room without windows where visitors are alone with their own selves. It is worth making a detour to shaft 1/2/8, where the former shower and changing rooms for the miners is home to *Pact Zollverein*, which was created through the merger of two dance ensembles, Projekt Tanzlandschaft Ruhr and Choreographisches Zentrum NRW.

From here there is a view of a grey cuboid building, an architectural masterpiece by the japanese architects office SANAA. Its conspicuous feature is a concentration of windows of different sizes at opposite corners, which blurs the boundaries between the floors. Together with the new university building called Quartier Nord for the faculty of design, it makes up the Folkwang Zollverein World Heritage Campus.

Turning from shaft XII to the coking plant, it is necessary to cross the *slag heap*. Nature has reclaimed the space between all these industrial buildings, allowing a habitat for rare plants and animals to emerge. By means of careful management of nature, *Zollverein Park* has been created with new paths, quiet zones and places to view art or play. This was possible thanks to an "artistic occupation" of the site in 1992 by Ulrich Rückriem, who succeeded in preventing a waste tip from being established here. His ensemble of 24 blocks of granite as tall as a man still makes its mark on the area and symbolises the enormous impact of heavy industry on the landscape of the region.

The *Zollverein coking plant*, in which 10,000 tons of coal were once processed into coke each day,

is now a popular attraction for its art projects. An installation by the British light artists Speirs and Major turns the whole complex into an impressive work of art after dark, when it is bathed in blue and red light, as there has been a solar power plant of photovoltaic modules on the roof of the loading hall since 1999. In the former salt depot, the *Palace of Projects* by Ilya and Emilia Kabakov, an accessible spiral sculpture, invites visitors to enter a world of dreams and utopias.

Bullmannaue 11
◆ *Tue-Fri 11.30am-3pm, 5.30pm-midnight,*
Sat 1pm-midnight, Sun 11.30am- midnight

The coking plant is also a location for lots of fun activities: in summer there is a view of the Zollverein World Heritage Site from the Sonnenrad, a Ferris wheel (*Sat–Sun noon-6pm, May-Sept*) and an opportunity to cool off on warm days in the swimming pool (*noon-8pm, July-Aug*). In winter the attraction is the 150-metre-long ice rink in the shadow of the old coke furnaces.

Zeche Carl
Wilhelm-Nieswandt-Allee 100
(Altenessen)
▲ *Altenessen Mitte*
Tel. 0201/8344410
www.zechecarl.de

Mining dominated life in the Altenessen district for over 100 years. Following the closure of the last mine, a new concept for the utilisation of the Carl pit was also sought. A self-administrating culture centre was created on the grounds in the late 1970s. The most famous element is now the Carl colliery, which has meanwhile become an institution and it is now impossible to conceive of Essen's cultural life without it. Alongside revue, political satire and concerts, parties, readings and exhibitions also take place here.

until 5pm

Hotels

Whether you're on a business trip, a cultural jaunt or a short vacation, you'll find accommodation in all price categories and for all tastes.

Messe Essen

With more than 1,4 million visitors from around 150 countries and around 50 trade shows and exhibitions more than 110 days of the year, the Essen trade fair complex and exhibition company is among the top ten in Germany. With 110,000 square metres of display space in 18 exhibition halls and the Galeria, exhibitors and visitors can find abundant opportunity to exchange information and cultivate contacts.

Norbertstrasse
(Rüttenscheid)
▲ *Messe Essen*
Tel. 0201/72440
www.messe-essen.de

■ **ATLANTIC CONGRESS HOTEL MESSE ESSEN**★★★★
Norbertstr. 2a
45131 Essen (Rüttenscheid)
Tel. 0201/9462880
Fax: 0201/94628818
▲ Messe Ost/Grugahalle
www.atlantic-congress-hotel-messe-essen.de

One the Worldhotels first Class Collection directly apart from the congress center in the popular quarter Rütten-scheid.

■ **NOVUM HOTEL AROSA ESSEN** ★★★★
Rüttenscheider Strasse 149
(Rüttenscheid)
45130 Essen
Tel. 0201/72260
Fax: 0201/7226100
▲ Martinstrasse
www.novum-hotels.com

Business and conference hotel on the Rü, Essen's main boulevard, close to the Messe and the Grugapark.

■ **BEST WESTERN PLUS HOTEL YPSILON**★★★★
Müller-Breslau-Strasse 18c
45130 Essen (Rüttenscheid)
Tel. 0201/89690
Fax: 0201/8969100
▲ Paulinenstrasse
www.ypsilon.bestwestern.de

With rooms for women and suites with water beds, this comfortable hotel near the exhibition centre and Grugahalle is suited to every occasion.

■ **HOLIDAY INN EXPRESS ESSEN – CITY CENTRE**★★★
Thea-Leymann-Strasse 11
45127 Essen (West quarter)
Tel. 0201/10260
Fax: 0201/1026100
▲ Berliner Platz
www.ihg.com/holidayinnexpress

Right on the edge of the pedestrian zone next to the Limbecker Platz and Colosseum theatre, the hotel offers business travellers and vacationers ideal conditions for a restful stay.

■ **HOLIDAY INN ESSEN CITY CENTRE**★★★★
Frohnhauser Strasse 6
45127 Essen (West Quarter)
Tel. 0201/24070
Fax: 0201/2407240
▲ Berliner Platz
www.ihg.com/holidayinn

Conveniently located in the city centre, with the Colosseum and pedestrian zone reachable on foot, this hotel has every amenity.

Hotel „An der Gruga"

Hotel Maximilians

■ HOSTEL GASTHAUS NORDSTERN
Stoppenberger Strasse 20
45141 Essen
(North Quarter)
Tel. 0201/32081
Fax 0201 /0811
▲ Am Freistein
www.gasthaus-nordstern-essen.de

This centrally located hostel only a few minutes from the city centre is a family-run business with individual service.

■ HOTEL AN DER GRUGA***
Eduard-Lucas-Strasse 17
45131 Essen
(Rüttenscheid)
Tel. 0201/841180
Fax: 0201/8411869
▲ Florastrasse
www.grugahotel.de

Business hotel a few steps away from the exhibition grounds and the Gruga Hall.

■ HOTEL BREDENEY****
Theodor-Althoff-Strasse 5
45133 Essen
(Bredeney)
Tel. 0201/7690
Fax: 0201/7691143
▲ Sommerburgstrasse
www.hotel-bredeney.de

Elegant first-class-hotel on the outskirts of the Essen municipal forest with a direct link to the A 52 motorway.

■ HOTEL MAXIMILIANS***
Manfredstrasse 10
45131 Essen
(Holsterhausen)
▲ Florastrasse
Tel. 0201/450170
Fax 0201/4501799
www.hotelmaximilians.de

A tip for business travellers and weekend trippers a few steps from the Messe Essen: outside Art Nouveau, inside contemporary design, state-of-the-art technology and everything guests need for work and relaxation.

■ HOTEL IBIS ESSEN**
Hollestrasse 50
45127 Essen
Tel. 0201/24280
Fax: 0201/2428600
▲ Hollestrasse, Essen Hbf.
www.ibis.com

Modern hotel in the city center next to the main station.

■ INTERCITYHOTEL ESSEN****
Hachestr. 10
45127 Essen (city centre)
Tel. 0201/8218410
Fax 0201/821841200
▲ Essen Hbf.
www.essen.intercityhotel.de

This newly opened four-star accommodation in the heart of the commercial district is an ideal base for business appointments and exploring the Capital of Culture.

Belle de Nuit
Messehaus West, the west wing designed by the Italian Mario Bellini, is an architectural highlight of the exhibition grounds. Thanks to the new light installation in the form of a ship's bows, the building looks especially good at night. With an area of 17,000 square metres and a

length of over 230 metres, Halle 3 is one of the largest unsupported halls in Europe. Thanks to the adjacent Grugapark (➤ p. 51), the site is an unusual venue for events. The attraction of the Galeria is Jörg Immendorf's glass work of art with the indicative title "Energy". It not only plays on Essen's significance as an energy industry location but also refers to the eco-friendly solar roof of the hall.

Hotels

**Landmarks:
Schurenbachhalde**
The 50-metre climb up the "Halde" (coal tailing pile or dump) is rewarded with a view over Essen, Gelsenkirchen and Bottrop. At least as impressive, however, is the "Bramme für das Ruhrgebiet" ("Slab for the Ruhr") by the American artist Richard Serra: 15 metres high and weighing 67 tonnes, it towers into the sky amidst a bleak, moonlike landscape.

Emscherstrasse/Eickwinkelstrasse (Altenessen)
▲ *Nordsternstrasse*

■ **MERCURE HOTEL PLAZA ESSEN******
Bismarckstrasse 48–50
45128 Essen (South Quarter)
Tel. 0201/878580
Fax: 0201/87858700
▲ Philharmonie
www.mercure.com

Situated on Essen's Culture Trail and in the direct vicinity of the Museum Centre, the out onto the park-like inner courtyard.

■ **MINTROPS LAND HOTEL BURGALTENDORF******
Schwarzensteinweg 81
45289 Essen (Burgaltendorf)
Tel. 0201/571710
Fax: 0201/5717147
▲ Burgaltendorf/Burgruine
www.mmhotels.de

This hotel in the south of Essen on the Ruhr peninsula, a green oasis above the river, was designed as a imagined a modern-day castle.

■ **MINTROPS STADT HOTEL MARGARETHENHÖHE******
Steile Strasse 46
45149 Essen (Margarethenhöhe)

Tel. 0201/43860
Fax: 0201/4386100
▲ Laubenweg
www.mmhotels.de

Stylish hotel nestling amidst the charming garden city of the same name.

■ **PARKHAUS HÜGEL*****
Freiherr-vom-Stein-Strasse 209
45133 Essen (Bredeney)
Tel. 0201/471091
Fax: 0201/444207

Sheraton

▲ Essen-Hügel
www.imhoff-essen.de

Romantic hotel directly beneath the Villa Hügel on the shores of Lake Baldeney.

■ **SCHLOSSHOTEL HUGENPOET*******
August-Thyssen-Strasse 51
45219 Essen (Kettwig)
Tel. 02054/12040
Fax: 02054/120450
▲ Kettwig Alter Bahnhof
www.hugenpoet.de

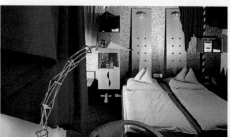
Mintrops Land Hotel

Schloss Hugenpoet

One of the "Leading Hotels of the World" is housed in a magnificent, moated late Renaissance manor house with a romantic park.

■ SHERATON ESSEN HOTEL*****
Huyssenallee 55
45128 Essen (South Quarter)
Tel. 0201/10070
Fax: 0201/1007777

Parkhaus Hügel

▲ Philharmonie
www.sheratonessen.com

The only five-star hotel in the city centre, but on the edge of the Stadtgarten park.

■ TOP CCL HOTEL ESSENER HOF****
Am Handelshof 5
45127 Essen (city centre)
Tel. 0201/24250
Fax: 0201/2425751
▲ Essen Hbf.
www.essener-hof.com

Like an oasis of peace and tranquillity, the leafy inner courtyard forms the centrepiece of the hotel, which is situated in a central yet quiet location in the city centre.

■ WEBERS – DAS HOTEL IM RUHRTURM***
Huttropstr. 60
45138 Essen
Tel. 0201/17003300
Fax: 0201/17003333
▲ Huttropstrasse
www.webershotel.de

Privately run business and congress hotel with boarding apartments, in a central location near the shopping centre and exhibition grounds.

■ WELCOME HOTEL ESSEN****
Schützenbahn 58
45127 Essen (city centre)
Tel. 0201/17790
Fax: 0201/1779199
▲ Rathaus Essen
www.welcome-hotel-essen.de

A luxurious business hotel in the heart of the city and the ideal base for visitors to trade fairs and events.

Schloss Borbeck
A trip to this moated castle, which dates back to about 1360, is a chance to relax and enjoy cultural and culinary treats. The former residence of the noble abbesses of Essen, which gained its late Baroque form through alterations in the 18th century, lies at the centre of exten-

sive parkland. Visitors can see a permanent exhibition about the history of the castle (Tue-Sun 2pm-6pm), listen to concerts, see an art exhibition or indulge in fine dining on the idyllic outdoor terrace.

Schlossstrasse 101 (Borbeck)
◆ Tue-Sun 11am-10pm
▲ Schloss Borbeck
Ticket reservations and info 0201/8844219
www.schloss-borbeck.essen.de

Cafes and Lunch

Feel like a cappuccino or a bite to eat after your sightseeing tour or stroll through the city centre? The various cafes and restaurants in the centre or in the suburbs are always good for a short refreshing stop!

Essen calendar

January
Essen on Ice (until February), JOE Jazzfestival

March
Equitana (every 2 years)

April
Essen Easter market, Easter fair at Borbeck Castle, Tour de Rü (oldtimer procession)

May
Frohnhauser May (city festival), Ruhr Piano Festival (till August)

June
Rü Festival, Extra Shift – Night of Industrial Culture, Ruhr European Classic Festival (till October), Cultural Trail Festival, comtemporary art ruhr

■ CAFÉ EXTRABLATT ESSEN
Kennedyplatz 5 (city centre)
▲ Hirschlandplatz
◆ Mon-Sat from 8am, Sun from 9am

A relax zone on the shopping mile with around 200 outdoor seats.

■ CAFÉ LIVRES
Moltkestrasse 2a (Moltkeviertel)
▲ Moltkestrasse
◆ Tue-Fri 9am-9pm, Sat-Sun 10am-9pm

This lovely French-style café for reading and literature has delicious things to give you a muffin top and is a wonderful spot for relaxing.

■ CRIOLLA – KLEINE PÂTISSERIE
Emmastrasse 7 (Rüttenscheid)
▲ Martinstrasse
◆ Wed-Fri 1-6pm, Sat 10am-2pm

In this Columbian patisserie you simply can't get enough of the cupcakes, which come in flavours such as Bourbon vanilla, passion fruit and strawberry, chocolate and many others.

■ CAFÉ KÖTTER
Rüttenscheider Strasse 73 (Rüttenscheid)
▲ Rüttenscheider Stern
◆ Mon-Sat 8am-7pm, Sun 9am-9pm

If you prefer to have your breakfast or some coffee and cake with no trendy people in sight, this is the right place!

■ CAFÉ SOLO
Kettwiger Strasse 36 (city centre)
▲ Hirschlandplatz
◆ Mon-Sat from 8.30am, Sun from 9am

See and be seen: street café in the Lichtburg invites you to spend some time here and watch the people going by.

■ CAFÉ SPRENGER
Frankenstr. 282 (Stadtwald)
▲ Stadtwald
◆ 8am-6pm

Try the superb quality of the cakes and pastries at this café on Stadtwaldplatz by the woods, where the eye-catcher is a show patisserie on the ground floor.

■ **CAPOBIANCO**
Rottstrasse 7 (city centre)
▲ Porscheplatz
◆ noon-11pm

Come here to enjoy home-made pasta, fish and meat dishes in Roman-style surroundings reminiscent of the Capella Sistina.

■ **I AM LOVE**
Moltkestrasse 3
(Moltkeviertel)
▲ Moltkestraße
◆ 9am-9pm

A kiosk where you can order home-made ice-cream and milk shakes, with tried-and-tested or experimental flavours to sample.

■ **KABÜ**
Annastrasse 51
(Rüttenscheid)
▲ Rüttenscheider Stern
◆ Mon-Fri 10am-7pm

Kabü stands for Kaffee (coffee) and Büro (office): here you can work while drinking delicious coffee and having hand-made cake.

■ **MIAMAMIA**
Rüttenscheider Strasse 183
(Rüttenscheid)
▲ Martinstrasse
◆ 9am-10pm

This is a great place to take a break and refresh yourself with delicious cappuccino, biscotti, panini, bruschette, tiramisu and many more Italian specialities – in the garden, if the weather is good.

■ **MONDRIAN**
Rüttenscheider Strasse 113
(Rüttenscheid)
▲ Rüttenscheider Stern
◆ Mon-Sat 9.30am-8pm

A coffee, espresso or cocktail in a chic setting: full breakfast + newspaper in the morning, lunches at midday, and bar and lounge in the evenings.

■ **MÖRCHENS EIS**
Rüttenscheider Str. 202
(Rüttenscheid)
▲ Florastrasse
◆ 10am-10.30pm

Hand-made ice cream. Danger of addiction!

■ **SWEET COFFEE PIRATES**
Rüttenscheider Strasse 218
(Rüttenscheid)
Tel. 0201/95984575
◆ Tue-Sat 9am-6pm,
Sun 10am-6pm

A coffee roaster with a coffee bar attached, where you can fill up with homemade cake, chocolate and other temptations.

Essen calendar

July
Essen verwöhnt ("Essen spoils you"), Summer Festival on the Gruga, Borbeck Castle Park Festival

August
Ruhr Triennale (till October), Essen Original, Grugapark Festival

September
Restaurant Carousel (til October), Borbeck Market Festival, Essen Sailing Week, Ludgerus Festival in Werden, Altenessener District Festival, "Großes Zechenfest"

October
Essen Light Weels (till January), International Spieltage Spiel (exhibition of play), innogy Marathon

November
Fashion Home Handicrafts (consumer fair), Essen Motor Show, comtemporary art ruhr

December
International Christmas Market

Restaurants

If you're a curried sausage and chips fan, you'll have to search a little longer. Alongside choice gourmet temples, what you'll find in Essen is a colourful and varied range of culinary delights!

Essen in figures

Essen lies in the middle of the Rhein-Ruhr region, one of the largest economic zones in Europe. More than eleven million people live and work here. With just about 590,000 inhabitants, Essen is not just the second-largest city in the Ruhr region but also one of the major German cities. The proportion of non-German citizens in the self-governing city within the Düsseldorf administrative district is 10.1 percent.

The city covers over 210 square kilometres and is divided into 9 urban regions and 50 municipal districts. The largest extension of the city precincts is 21 kilometres in the North-South direction and 17 kilo-metres in the West-East direction. The highest elevation is 202.5 metres, the lowest is 26.5 metres above sea level.

■ DER BONNER HOF "BIENVENIDOS"
Kringsgat 14 (Kettwig)
Tel. 02054/5386
▲ Kettwiger Markt
◆ Thu-Sun 11.30am-2.30pm, 5-11pm

If you like a Spanish atmosphere, this is the place – come and enjoy Spanish-German fusion cuisine.

■ GRILL ROOM BISTECCA
Rüttenscheiderstrasse 2 (Rüttenscheid)
Tel. 0201/74716931
▲ Bismarckplatz
◆ Mon-Fri noon-3pm, Mon-Sat 6pm-11am

For everyone who loves beef, this upmarket steakhaus in the Glückauf-haus next to the Filmstudio, which was modelled on the great grill rooms of New York, is first choice.

■ HANNAPPEL
Dahlhauser Strasse 173 (Horst)
Tel. 0201/534506
▲ Breloher Steig
◆ Mon, Wed-Sat 5.30-11pm, Sun 11.30am-3pm, 5.30-10pm

Top culinary address in a former corner pub on the city's border with Bochum.

■ HUGENPÖTTCHEN
(in Schlosshotel Hugen-poet)
August-Thyssen-Strasse 51 (Kettwig)
Tel. 02054/12040
▲ Kettwig Alter Bahnhof
◆ noon-11pm

Restaurant in the conservatory of the palace, with creative country-house cuisine and an idyllic terrace in the courtyard.

■ JAGDHAUS SCHELLENBERG
Heisinger Strasse 170a (Stadtwald)
Tel. 0201/437870
▲ Schöne Aussicht
◆ Tue-Sat noon-3pm, 6pm-1am, Sun noon-1am

The restaurant is not just worth a visit because of its historic half-timbered architecture and its fantastic view over Lake Baldeney, it also has fine food on offer. The Quick-Lunch can be re-commended to lunch guests in a hurry.

■ LA GRAPPA
Rellinghauser Strasse 4 (South quarter)
Tel. 0201/231766

Esszimmer

![Bruschetta Pizze Vini Pasta](header image)

▲ Hauptbahnhof
◆ Mon-Fri 11.30am-2.30pm
+ 5.30-11.30pm,
Sat 5.30-11.30pm

Your host Rino Frattesi and his team cook up the finest Italian meals.

■ MONGO'S
Altendorfer Strasse 3a
(city centre)
Tel. 0201/1095986
▲ Berliner Platz
◆ Mon-Thu 5pm-midnight,
Fri 4pm-1am, Sat noon-1pm,
Sun 11.30am-midnight

Asian cuisine of a different kind: each guest chooses the meal from the buffet and then has it cooked! Indeed a culinary experience.

PAUL'S BRASSERIE
Huyssenallee 7
(South quarter)
Tel. 0201/26675976
▲ Hauptbahnhof
◆ Tue-Fri noon-3pm,
6-11pm

An elegant restaurant with traditional French specialities.

■ PELAYO
Rüttenscheider Strasse 138
(Rüttenscheid)
Tel. 0201/779782

▲ Martinstrasse
◆ 5pm-11pm

The in-place for lovers of Spanish tapas cuisine in high quality.

■ ROTISSERIE DU SOMMELIER
Wegener Strasse 3
(Rüttenscheid)
Tel. 0201/9596930
▲ Martinstrasse
◆ Tue-Sat noon-3pm,
6pm-midnight

Let chef and sommelier Thomas Friedrich spoil you in true French style in his charming restaurant with the atmosphere of an upscale bistro: French cuisine and an outstanding wine list.

■ SCHIFFERS IM ALTEN LÖWEN
Brückstrasse 20 (Werden)
Tel. 0201/84850597
▲ Werden
◆ Tue-Fri noon-2pm,
Tue-Sat 6-11pm

A small eatery with a beer garden and a changing food menu, according to the motto "simply good cooking with no frills".

■ TABLO
Huyssenallee 5
(South Quarter)
Tel. 0201/8119585
▲ Hauptbahnhof,
Aalto-Theater
◆ Mon-Thu 11am-11.30pm,
Fri-Sat 11am-midnight, Sun
noon-11.30pm

Eyecatching decoration: Turkish in-restaurant with Gault Millau points.

Essen in figures

Essen can boast a first-class climate for education and training: more than 300 different institutes, the city forms the heart of the densest training and research landscape in the world. Over 70,000 students are enrolled at the 3 universities with their different locations. The city has optimal medical facilities: More than 5,500 beds are available in 15 hospitals. With 80 hotels and other forms of lodging and over about 9,000 beds, Essen can offer all kinds of accommodation in categories from "straight-forward" to "luxury". The metropolis heads the accommodation statistics in the Ruhr region with over 1,400,000 overnight stays, including 145,000 from visitors outside Germany.

In the cultural domain Essen can point to a gigantic range of offerings: around 20 museums can be visited and in the evening more than 20 theatres and concert halls and 8 cinemas offer a full spectrum of entertainment.

Pubs and Beer Gardens

Enjoying the sunset from within old industrial walls, drinking a Pilsner in a stand-up bar or bopping in the pubs along Essen's amusement mile, the Rü – there's a host of different ways to go out.

Ampütte

geöffnet
18⁰⁰-4⁰⁰ Uhr

Savouring Essen

The Ruhr metropolis invites its citizens and visitors to savour its culinary delights twice a year: in June top gastronomic establishments pitch their tents for four days along the Gourmet Mile in the city centre with the intention of spoiling the public with tasty delicacies. It's then the turn of the Restaurant Carousel from September to October: the city's kitchen chefs open up their restaurants to offer a four-course meal with a choice of two main dishes at a palatable price. The great thing about it: the wine's already included!

www.essengeniessen.de

■ **11 FREUNDE - DIE BAR**
Kunigundastrasse 27/corner of Girardetstrasse (Rüttenscheid)
▲ Paulinenstrasse
◆ Tue-Fri from 7pm, Sat from 2pm, Sun from 3pm

Football pub in 1970s style where fans can watch matches on several LCD TVs and screens. To go with it there's typical „stadium food", from Hertha's curry sausage and French fries to Fortuna meatballs.

■ **ANYWAY**
Berliner Strasse 82 (Frohnhausen)
▲ Gervinusstrasse
◆ Wed-Sun from 7pm

A cult pub for music with a programme of concerts, and communal viewing of the "Tatort" TV thriller on Sundays.

■ **„DAMPFE"/ GASTHOF BORBECK**
Heinrich-Brauns-Strasse 9-15 (Borbeck)
▲ Borbeck Bahnhof
◆ Mon-Thu 11am-11pm, Fri-Sat 11am-1am, Sun 10.30am-11pm

Pub run by the Borbeck steam beer brewery with a large terrace under giant trees.

■ **HAUS AM SEE**
Harnscheidts Höfe 1 (Bredeney)
▲ Heskämpchen
◆ Fri 2-10pm, Sat-Sun noon-10pm

A tip for when the sun shines: a country house with a large beer garden in the middle of the nature reserve on Baldeneysee.

■ **LE CHAT NOIR**
Birgittastrasse 22 (Rüttenscheid)
▲ Rüttenscheider Stern
◆ from 6pm

Wine bar with a selection of meals and cheese boards. Come on Saturday morning for the hangover breakfast.

■ **LEO'S CASA**
Kennedyplatz 7 (city centre)
▲ Hirschlandplatz
◆ Mon-Fri from 11am, Sat from 10am, Sun from 1pm

This cosy tavern in the Europahaus is worth a stop nut just after Dr. Stratmann's programme of medical satire.

■ LUKAS

(Culinary Rail Station)
Prinz-Friedrich-Strasse 1
(Kupferdreh)
▲ Kupferdreh Bahnhof
◆ Tue-Fri from 5pm, Sat
from 1pm, Sun from 10am

Restaurant and beer
garden within the old walls
of the Kupferdreh railway
station.

■ MITTENDRINN

Klarastrasse 70 (Rüttenscheid)
▲ Cäcilienstrasse
◆ Mon-Sat from 5pm,
Sun from 10am

Gastropub – something
between a pub and a
restaurant with a beer
garden in the centre of
Rüttenscheid.

■ PLAN B

Rüttenscheider Strasse 201
(Rüttenscheid)
▲ Martinstrasse
◆ from 11am

The in-place to be, but
also somewhere to enjoy
an excellent meal or drink
coffee during the day.

■ RÜTTENSCHEIDER HAUSBRAUEREI

Girardetstrasse 2-38
(Rüttenscheid)
▲ Martinstrasse
◆ Tue-Thu 5pm-midnight,
Fri-Sat 5pm-1am, Sun-Mon
5-11pm

Here's well-brewed beer to
savour, freshly drawn from
oak barrels both indoors
and outdoors.

■ SEASIDE BEACH BALDENEY

Freiherr-von-Stein-Strasse
84 (Bredeney)
▲ Villa Hügel
◆ from 10am (in good
weather)

For a cocktail at the bar or
a tasty barbecue – a trip
to this South Sea paradise
in the south of Essen is
always worthwhile.

■ SPIESSER

Rüttenscheider Straße 214
(Rüttenscheid)
▲ Florastraße
◆ Mon-Sat 11.30am-3pm,
5.30-10pm

A wine bistro with an at-
tractive garden on the Rü.

■ UNPERFEKTHAUS

Friedrich-Ebert-Strasse 18
▲ Berliner Platz
◆ Mon-Thu 7am-11pm,
Fri-Sat 7am-1am,
Sun 8am -11pm

In this unusual artists' vil-
lage with an area of 4,000
square metres, you can
watch creative people at
work, be creative yourself,
buy a gift and have a bite
to eat in the restaurant at
all-inclusive prices.

■ WASSERGARTEN

Lührmannstraße 70
▲ Messe Ost/Gruga
◆ 4-10pm (summer)

One of Essen's most beauti-
ful beergardens amidst
the idyllic backdrop of the
Grugapark.

Refreshment stand as the place to meet

They're mostly not
exactly pretty to look
at, but they have a firm
place in the hearts of
people in the local-
ity: the Trinkhallen or
refreshment booths
that belong to the Ruhr
region like the curried
sausage belongs to
chips with ketchup and
mayonnaise. Here, one
not only buys what one
has forgotten but also
tells a life story or two.
These "kiosks on the
corner" emerged 100
years ago as a meeting-
place for the miners
and steel workers after
their shifts had ended.
They're hardly any
mines these days, but
the drinking halls have
remained.

Bars & Nightlife

How about winding up the evening with a cocktail or dancing the night away? These are the places to check out!

"I think they'll be coming to get me"

Everybody knows him in Germany, the early retired character from the Ruhr who has to throw in his two cents worth even though he mostly hasn't the foggiest idea what he's talking about. His characteristic guise is thick shell-rimmed glasses, "Prince-Heinrich

cap", beige granddad jacket and trousers at halfmast. When Uwe Lyko alias Herbert Knebel and his "Affentheater" band (Martin Breuer, Georg Göbel, Detlef Hinze) take the stage, nobody's safe from a slating. The stories spun in the above-named comedy programme not only centre around Guste, "her indoors", but also wittily relate all the chicanery and catastrophes the world has to offer.

■ FILOU DANCE CLUB

Pferdemarkt 2-4 (city centre)
▲ Rheinischer Platz, Viehofer Platz
◆ Wed 7pm-4am, Fri-Sat 8pm-5am

For the after-job party on Wednesdays or another of the party nights, this club is one of the hotspots in Essen's nightlife.

■ BANDITEN WIE WIR

Kahrstrasse 3 (Rüttenscheid)
▲ Rüttenscheider Stern
◆ Tue-Sat from 8pm

This bar is a hotspot in Essen's nightlife. Readings and small concerts also take place.

■ BAR AM PARK (IM SHERATON ESSEN HOTEL)

Huyssenallee 55 (South Quarter)
▲ Philharmonie/Saalbau
◆ 10-1am

Essen's only daytime bar, with stylish décor. In summer the big terrace in the Stadtgarten park is an inviting venue.

■ CLUB ESSENCE

Viehofer Strasse 38-52 (city centre)
▲ Viehofer Platz
◆ Sat from 11pm

Popular club in what was once a cinema, where you can hit the dance floor or relax in the Secret Lounge.

■ DELTA MUSIK PARK

Frohnhauser Strasse 75 (West End)
▲ Westendstrasse
◆ Fri-Sat and evening of public holidays from 10pm

The grand-daddy of all the clubs in Essen is a stylish location where you can party on several floors in the halls of what used to be a Krupp factory. Immaculate dress is obligatory!

■ HANS DAMPF

Zweigertstrasse 12 (Passage, Rüttenscheid)
▲ Rüttenscheider Stern
◆ Fri-Sat from 11pm

A club for chilling at the bar or dancing to pop, hiphop, disco, rock or dance classics.

■ HOTEL SHANGHAI

Steeler Strasse 33 (city centre)
▲ Rathaus
◆ Fri-Sat from 11pm

Club with a non-mainstream programme!

Maze

Baliha Dance Club

◾ LUCY
Rüttenscheider Stern 1
(Rüttenscheid)
▲ Rüttenscheider Stern
◆ Fri-Sat from 11pm

Trendy club in Essen's party district in the style of the burlesque 1920s with a big cocktail bar and dance floor.

◾ MENEHUNE BAR
Wehmenkamp 3
(Rüttenscheid)
▲ Martinstrasse
◆ Wed-Thu 7pm-1am, Fri-Sat 7pm-4am

Cosy bar in Caribbean style, one of the best places in town for cocktails.

◾ PEDROS CUBA LOUNGE
Rüttenscheider Strasse 319
(Rüttenscheid)
▲ Alfredusbad
◆ from 6pm

Cuban lounge where you can wear out your dancing shoes at the weekend salsa parties.

◾ TEMPLE BAR
Salzmarkt 1 (city centre)
▲ Hirschlandplatz
◆ from 4pm

An old-established favourite in the Essen bar scene: come to chill out upstairs, or at weekend for hot beats down in the cellar.

◾ STOFFWECHSEL
Hedwigstrasse 5
(Rüttenscheid)
▲ Rüttenscheider Stern
◆ Tue-Fri 4pm-1.30am, Sat from 11am

Lovingly designed bar with retro charm, an ideal rendezvous.

◾ ZECHE CARL
Wilhelm-Nieswandt-Allee 100
(Altenessen)
▲ Altenessen-Mitte

This place really throbs on Fridays and Saturdays: Cantilene Swingball, 80s New German Wave, or a Gothic-Industrial party.
*Programme: see
www.zechecarl.de*

Techno Classica
... is a must in the diary of every oldtimer enthusiast. For four whole days Essen's exhibition halls are totally devoted to classic cars and motorcycles, their spare parts and restoration, clubs, museums, models, accessories, and everything else that sends the oldtimer fans' pulses racing. More than 1,250 exhibitors over 110,000 square metres, around 2,500 dolled-up automobile gems in 20 exhibition halls and more than 190,000 visitors each year make this event the world's largest classic car show.
www.siha.de

Wellness + Health

For those who want to do something positive for their wellbeing or simply relax and take it easy, Essen offers an extensive spectrum of opportunities to pamper yourself and feel good – from steam baths, Finnish saunas and saltwater inhalation to a preventive medical check-up.

Just like on holiday: Lake Baldeney

One of the loveliest and largest local recreation areas lies to the south of the Ruhr metropolis. The the approximately 2.7-square-kilometre lake with a circuit of 14.7 kilometres was created between 1931 and 1933 by damming the River Ruhr and is scenically situated amidst a forest-covered hill landscape. Those of you who aren't into hiking, cycling, inline skating or jogging should definitely take a trip to the lake's own White Fleet of boats.

Weisse Flotte Baldeney GmbH Tel. 0201/5024713 www.flotte-essen.de

■ ALTE BADEANSTALT
Altenessener Strasse 393 (Altenessen)
Tel. 0201/8331196
▲ Altenessen-Mitte
◆ Mon-Fri 7-10am, Mon-Tue, Thu-Fri 3-6pm, Sat 7am-1pm
www.essenerbaeder.de

Here you can relax in the Sauna-Wellness-Park or work out in the Fitness-Club.

■ BODYGUARD!
Centre for preventive medicine at the Elisabeth-Krankenhaus Essen
Herwarthstrasse 102 (South Quarter)
Tel. 0201/8973901
Fax: 0201/8973909
▲ Wörthstrasse
www.bodyguard-essen.de

Individual check-ups for companies and on a private basis: in an extremely short period of time (generally within a day), the team conducts an individually tailored programme of medical examinations from various specialist disciplines.

■ GOLFCLUB HEIDHAUSEN
Preutenborbeckstrasse 36 (Heidhausen)
Tel. 0201/404111
▲ Grenze Heidhausen
www.gceh.de

Those looking to relax with a round of golf and who are up to will find a lovely 27-hole course in Heidhausen on the edge of the Ruhr area.

■ GRUGAPARK THERME
Lührmannstrasse 70 (Rüttenscheid)
Tel. 0201/856100
▲ Messe-Ost/Gruga or Messe West/Süd/Gruga
◆ Mon-Thu 8.30am-9pm, Fri-Sat 8.30am-10pm, Sun 9am-6.30pm
Grugaparktherme: Mon-Thu 9am-10pm, Fri 9am-11pm, Sun 9am-7pm
grugaparktherme.de

The Grugapark is to Essen what Central Park is to New York and the Boboli gardens to Florence, but with a difference: it also has a spa right in the city! Here you can take a sauna in the Grugapark baths, inhale the healthy salt air in the Gradierwerk, benefit from Kneipp treatments or just recover from the stress of everyday routine with a soothing massage.

■ LET'S FEEL!
Gutenbergstrasse 17-19 (South Quarter)
Tel. 0201/7474884
▲ Aalto-Theater
◆ Mon, Thu 5–7 pm, Tue 10am-1pm, Wed, Fri 10–noon, 4-8pm, Sat 10am-noon
www.salzgrotte.net

Ronald McDonald Haus

On the edge of the Grugapark stands an unusual building in a style that was inspired by a volcanic crater and a protective cave. Friedensreich Hundertwasser's last project before his death in February 2000 was to design a family centre for the McDonald's Children's Foundation: the relatives of children who are seriously ill are offered a temporary home in this "humanitarian oasis" while the children are being treated in the Essen university clinic.

Unterm Sternenzelt 1 (Holsterhausen),
▲ Holsterhauser Platz, www.mcdonalds-kinderhilfe.org

Relaxation to the sound of music in a sea salt grotto: the combination of seawater and rock salts creates microclimatic conditions that are nowhere else to be found.

■ PREVENTICUM GMBH
Clinic for diagnostics and medical consultation
Theodor-Althoff-Strasse 47 (Bredeney)
Tel. 0201/847170
Fax: 0201/8471722
▲ Karstadt Hauptverwaltung
www.preventicum.de

Within 4 hours you can find out more about your physical constitution: this spin-off company from the University of Essen carries out your own personal health check-up in an absolutely discrete environment using state-of-the-art examination techniques.

■ SEASIDE BEACH BALDENEY
Freiherr-vom-Stein-Strasse 384 (Bredeney)
Tel. 0201/49060949
▲ Villa Hügel
◆ 10am-10pm (if the weather's fine)
www.seaside-beach-baldeney.de

A short break shaded by palms: Play a game of beach volleyball, enjoy a massage under palm trees or simply relax over a cocktail at the beach bar – whatever you want to do, the Beach Club on the shores of Lake Baldeney offers many ways to relax.

Green oasis: Grugapark
Whoever visits the landscaped park with its old stock of trees will be astounded once again by the abundance of green in this supposedly grey part of the world. The Grugapark grew out of the Ruhr Horticultural Exhibition in 1929 and is now one of the largest European parkland and leisure areas with an area of 700,000 square metres. It is home to exotic animals and plant species from across the globe. It's not just a source of relaxation for the citizens, but also serves as the backdrop for concerts, exhibitions and summer festivals.

Külshammerweg 32
Tel. 0201/8883106
▲ Essen Gruga
◆ 9am till dark
www.grugapark.de

Culture

There is good reason why Essen is one of the important places of the the Capital of Culture 2010: the regular evening programme of cultural offerings is bursting at the seams with drama and cabaret, variety and music hall, revue, musicals, music and movies.

Gruga Hall

The "concrete butter-fly", as the Grugahalle is affectionately known among the citizens, has been a fixed element in the cultural landscape of the Rhein-Ruhr basin for almost six decades now. The landmark, which is known far beyond the city boundaries, is alternately a stage and auditorium for stars and orchestras, a sports venue, circus arena, ice palace or convention hall, and it presents great names from throughout the world. More than 200,000 visitors attend around 70 events each year.

Norbertstrasse (Rüttenscheid) Tickets 0201/7244290
▲ *Messe-Ost/Gruga*
www.grugahalle.de

Music & dance

■ AALTO-THEATER

Opernplatz 10 (South Quarter)
Tel.: 0201/8122200
▲ Aalto-Theater
www.aalto-musiktheater.de

This is not just an architectural gem. The Aalto-Theater accommodates the Aalto-Musiktheater, which is directed by Stefan Soltesz and was voted "Opera House of the Year" in 2008; the Essen Philharmonic Orchestra, which also won an award in 2008 as "Best Orchestra"; and the Aalto Ballett Theater Essen, directed by Ben Van Cauwenbergh, which has been the best regional ballet ensemble for years.

■ BRUNEL. TANZ. CIE.

Programme: see list of venues at
www.brunel-tanzcie.com

Most of the work of the Folkwang pupil Christine Brunel consists of solos, duets and quintets. Her choreography conceives of the body as an instrument, and movement as a kind of music in the context of space and time.

■ BÜRGERMEISTERHAUS

Heckstrasse 105 (Werden)
Tel. 0201/493286
▲ Werden-Markt
www.buergermeisterhaus.de

The sounds of classical, jazz or tango music can be enjoyed in this 19th-century villa as in a salon for aes thetes. Poetry evenings, cabaret and exhibitions are also staged.

■ COLOSSEUM THEATER

Altendorfer Strasse 1 (West End)
Tel. 0201/24020
▲ Berliner Platz
www.colosseumtheater.de

Musical theatre in an impressive historic ambience: in the listed industrial hall, which once formed the gateway to "Krupp City", famous musicals are dancing across the stage.

■ FOLKWANG UNIVERSITÄT DER KÜNSTE

Klemensborn 39 (Werden)
Tickets 0201/4903231
▲ Werden Markt
www.folkwang-uni.de

Extensive programme of events from musicals, opera, drama, pantomime and dance to instrumental, choral, orchestral, jazz and computer music.

■ PACT ZOLLVEREIN CHOREOGRAPHISCHES ZENTRUM NRW
Bullmannaue 20 (Stoppenberg)
Tel: 0201/8122200
▲ Abzweig Katernberg
www.pact-zollverein.de

A delight for fans of contemporary dance: the Choreographische Zentrum NRW presents international dance productions including world, European and German premieres.

■ PHILHARMONIE ESSEN
Huyssenallee 53 (South Quarter)
Tel. 0201/8122200
▲ Philharmonie/Saalbau
www.philharmonie-essen.de

After being completely renovated, the Philharmonie was given a festive reopening in 2004. Today it is the base of the Essener Philharmoniker (Essen Philharmonic Orchestra). The high-class programme ranges from symphony, chamber and choral music to evenings of jazz and new music.

Theatre

■ DAS KLEINE THEATER
Gänsemarkt 42 (city centre)
Tickets 0201/5209852
▲ Berliner Platz
www.kleines-theater-essen.de

Essen's oldest private theatre plays demanding boulevard comedies and plays. Guest productions and youth theatre performances round off the offerings.

■ ESSENER VOLKSBÜHNE E.V.
Tickets: *vorverkauf@ essener-volksbuehne.de*
Playing schedule and locations: *www.essener-volksbuehne.de*

One of the oldest surviving amateur stages in Germany, whose repertoire embraces everything from boulevard theatre to fairy-tales.

RuhrTriennale
The industrial monuments of the region are the stage for an international festival of the arts in the Ruhr area, a multi-genre event which has had great success since 2002 under the title RuhrTriennale. The performances enter into a dialogue with the character of the individual venues. In former factory halls and sites such as the coking plant in Essen, theatre and opera are combined with innovative trends in the visual arts, pop music and concerts. The artistic direction of the festival changes on a three-year cycle: in the years 2018-2021 the sixth RuhrTriennale will be directed by Stefanie Carp, who thus follows in the footsteps of Gerard Mortier, Jürgen Flimm, Willy Decker, Heiner Goebbels and Johan Simons.

Tel. 0221/280210
www.ruhrtriennale.de

53

Culture

Essen.Original
What started more than 10 years ago as a one-day party on the occasion of the city's 100-year jubilee has meanwhile become an institution: the city celebrates a gigantic open-air culture festival for three days every summer. Rock & pop, classic, jazz, hip hop, techno, German pop hits and comedy fill the programme that presents various stars and would-be stars. An unmistakable emblem of this cultural marathon is the silhouettes created by the designer Bernward Kraft, who comes up with a new motif each year.

www.essen-original.de

■ **FREUDENHAUS – THEATER IM GREND**
Westfalenstrasse 311 (Steele)
Tickets 0201/8513230
▲ Grendplatz, Steele-S-Bahnhof
www.theater-freudenhaus.de

Theatre in the GREND Cultural Centre, which has made a name for itself far beyond the region with its Ruhr region comedies. The theatre also offers chanson evenings and a diverse programme of other shows.

■ **GOP VARIETÉ**
Rottstrasse 30 (city centre)
Tel. 0201/2479393
▲ Viehofer Platz
www.variete.de

International variety theatre with juggling, magic, ventriloquism and acrobatics as well as excellent comedy elements.

■ **KATAKOMBEN-THEATER IM GIRARDETHAUS**
Girardetstrasse 2-38 (Rüttenscheid)
Tickets 0201/4304672
▲ Martinstrasse
www.katakomben-theater.de

Revue and political satire, jazz, (children's) theatre, World Music and dance make up the programme presented by the former Satiricon Theatre.

SCHAUSPIEL ESSEN:
■ **GRILLO-THEATER, HELDENBAR, CAFÉ CENTRAL**
Theaterplatz 11
■ **CASA, BOX**
Theaterplatz 7 (city centre)
Tickets 0201/8122200
▲ Hirschlandplatz
www.schauspiel-essen.de

The programme focuses on ambitious productions of classic dramas and contemporary works under the direction of Christian Tombeil. Three stages are available: the main stage of the Grillo-Theater, as well as Casa and Box for studio productions. In the Heldenbar of the Grillo-Theater, in addition to its normal function as a bar small-scale drama, dance and concerts are performed, and Café Central not only serves food but is also a venue for lectures, discussion forums and evenings of songs.

■ **STRATMANNS THEATER IM EUROPAHAUS ESSEN**
Kennedyplatz 7 (city centre)
Tickets 0201/8204060
▲ Hirschlandplatz
www.stratmanns.de

"The main thing is that I'll be helped" – the medical satire of Dr. Stratmann is widely known far beyond

the Ruhr metropolis. Since 1994 the former doctor turned satirist Dr. Stratmann has been staging a wide variety of events in his own Europahaus theatre, including comedies, English-language theatre, children's and puppet theatre, concerts, chanson evenings, and discussions.

■ STUDIO-BÜHNE ESSEN
Korumhöhe 11
(Kray-Leithe)
Tel. 0201/551505
▲ Wendelinstrasse
www.studio-buehne-essen.de

The Studio-Bühne is a fixed star in Essen's cultural firmament with its varied programme ranging from the traditional to the avant-garde.

■ THEATER COURAGE
Goethestrasse 67
(Rüttenscheid)
▲ Zweigertstrasse,
Rüttenscheider Stern
Tickets 0201/791466
www.theatercourage.de

Small-scale theatre, whose name evokes the tough problems successfully grappled with during the 1980/90s. Today, the venue specialises in such diverse entertainment as comedies, music revues, erotic readings, and talent shows.

■ THEATER IM RATHAUS
Porscheplatz/Rathaus
(city centre)
Tickets 0201/2455555
▲ Porscheplatz
www.theater-im-rathaus.de

Entertaining boulevard theatre with stars from film and television.

Cinemas

■ CINEMAXX ESSEN
Berliner Platz 4–5
(West End)
Tickets 040/80806969
▲ Berliner Platz
www.cinemaxx.de

Supermodern multiplex cinema showing all the current releases.

■ EULENSPIEGEL THEATER
Steeler Strasse 208–212
(Southeast)
▲ Wörthstrasse
Tickets 0201/275555
www.essener-filmkunsttheater.de

Art cinema with a programme that has won several prizes and a Wurlitzer silent movie organ.

Filmstudio Glückauf
Filmstudio, North Rhine-Wesphalia's oldest arthouse cinema, which was founded by the city of Essen in 1924 as a "reform cinema" and screened art films in contrast to the programme of pure entertainment at other cinemas, had had a stroke of luck: thanks to the efforts of director Marianna Menze, this home of cinematic culture will stay in the Glückaufhaus in the centre of Rüttenscheid. The 1920s office building, a listed monument with a brick façade, is rebuilt. The old auditorium with its original tilting seats, leather armchairs and wooden panelling is reconstructed, so that cinema-goers have again been able to enjoy the outstanding, multiple award-winning annual film programme.

Rüttenscheider Strasse 2 (Rüttenscheid)

tickets: 0201/43936633

www.essener-filmkunsttheater.de

Museums

From coal mining to modern art, from ethnology to mineralogy – whatever interests you, Essen's museums have it!

Galleries

Hardly anyone has prof-ited more from the structural change in the Ruhr region than the art scene: artists have moved into old works halls and museums have been opened in the industrial monuments. Under such conditions, it seems only natural that a lively gallery scene has emerged. The most famous galleries include Kunstraum (Rüttenscheider Strasse 56), Galerie Neher (Kaninchenberghöhe 8/ Rellinghausen), Galerie Obrist (Kahrstrasse 59/ Südviertel) and Galerie Schütte (Hauptstrasse 4/ Kettwig).

■ **DOMSCHATZKAMMER**
➤ p. 18

■ **PHÄNOMANIA ERFAHRUNGSFELD**
Am Handwerkerpark 8-10 (Zollverein colliery Shaft 3/7/10)
Tel. 0201/301030
▲ Huestrasse
◆ Mon-Fri 9am-6pm, Sat-Sun 10am-6pm
www.phaenomania.de

Permanent exhibition aiming at the activation of sensory perception.

■ **GALERIE IM KUNSTHAUS ESSEN E.V.**
Rübezahlstrasse 33 (Rellinghausen)
Tel. 0201/443313
▲ Annental
◆ Thu-Sun 3-6pm
www.kunsthaus-essen.de

Forum for exposure to contemporary art: regular exhibitions and inter-national projects with work in all media dealing with contem-porary issues.

■ **GALERIE IM SCHLOSS BORBECK**
Schlossstrasse 101 (Borbeck)
Tel. 0201/8844219
▲ Schloss Borbeck
◆ Thu-Sun 3-6pm

Exhibition programme at *www.schloss-borbeck.essen.de*

■ **KUNSTVEREIN RUHR E.V.**
Kopstadtplatz 12 (city centre)
Tel. 0201/226538

▲ Porscheplatz
◆ Tue-Fri noon-6pm,
Sat-Sun 2pm-5pm
www.kunstvereinruhr.de

An attraction way beyond
Essen due to its high-
calibre exhibitions.

■ MARKT- UND SCHAU-STELLERMUSEUM

Hachestrasse 68
(West Quarter)
Tel. 0179/2093054
▲ Hauptbahnhof
◆ on prior notification, free
www.schaustellermuseum.de

A unique collection of
exhibits from the domain
of carnies, markets and tra-
velling amusement shows.

■ MINERALIEN-MUSEUM

Kupferdreher Strasse 141-
143 (Kupferdreh)
Tel. 0201/24681444

▲ Kupferdreh, Poststrasse
oder Kupferdreher Markt
◆ Tue-Sun 10am-6pm,
www.ruhrmuseum.de

From the world of minerals:
an external site of the Ruhr
Museum in a 19th-century
former school building with
both permanent displays
and special exhibitions.

■ MUSEUM FOLKWANG
➤ p. 30

■ RUHR MUSEUM
➤ p. 34

■ RED DOT DESIGN MUSEUM
➤ p. 34

■ SOUL OF AFRICA MUSEUM

Rüttenscheider Strasse 36
(Rüttenscheid)
Tel. 0201/787640
▲ Rüttenscheider Stern
◆ Thu, Sat, Sun 2-6pm,
Fri 6-10pm
www.soul-of-africa.com

Collection of West African
art belonging to the
photojournalist Henning
Christoph, whose intention
it is to promote understanding of and kindle interest
in this misunderstood
culture.

■ VILLA HÜGEL
➤ p. 22

Berthold Beitz (1913-2013)

When Alfried Krupp
took over the manage-
ment of the Krupp
Company again in 1953
and renounced arma-
ments production, he
called on someone to
help him without whom

the resurgence of the
company would have
been inconceivable.
In the capacity of
chief executive and
super-visory board
chairman, Berthold
Beitz has steered
the fate of the Krupp
concern over decades.
After Alfried's death
1967, he transferred
the Krupp estate into
the AlfriedKrupp von
Bohlen und Halbach-
Stiftung and set up the
Ruhr Cultural Founda-
tion in 1984. The fact
that the former coal,
iron and steel region
is now a thriving
business, scientific and
cultural centre is also
thanks to his formative
vision and personal
commitment.

shopping

Fashion, design, gifts and souvenirs ... around the Kettwiger Strasse, Essen's main shopping mile, there's something in store for every taste. In the Rü and the other suburbs, the shopping's smaller-scale but no less interesting.

Essen Light Weeks
It's anything but dark in Essen during the dark times of the year: the sky above the city centre is brightly illuminated from the end of October onwards when countless light bulbs, kilometres of light tubes and tons of angular and sectional iron is formed into large-scale light images. What started as a "light show" over five decades ago is today a sophisticated major event. Since 2001 one of the EU partner states has been introduced each year in images of light and with cultural activities under the motto "Europe in Essen".

www.lichtwochen.essen.de

■ **3-ZIMMERKÜCHEBAD**
Rüttenscheider Strasse 211 (Rüttenscheid)
▲ Florastraße
◆ Mon-Fri 11am-7pm, Sat 11am-4pm

A concept store for home items and accessories in Scandinavian style, straightforward and functional with clear design reduced to essentials.

■ **DESIGNPALETTE AUF ZOLLVEREIN**
Halle 12, Studio 2
Altendorfer Strasse 11
▲ Zollverein
◆ Tue-Sun 11am-6pm

A market place for designers, craft workers and other creative talents. An area of more than 140 square metres is devoted to living accessories, jewellery, bags, hats, and arts and crafts.

■ **GABRIELE BENSE**
Gemarkenstrasse 60 (Holsterhausen)
▲ Gemarkenplatz
◆ Mon-Fri 10am-6pm, Sat 10am-1.30pm

Gift shop that combines tried-and-tested classics with modern trend-setting items.

■ **JOHNNYTAPETE – VINTAGE WALLPAPER**
Dinnendahlstrasse 8 (Huttrop)
Tel. 0201/6124647
▲ Dinnendahlstrasse
◆ on appointment

Highly unusual: original wallpaper from the fifties, sixties and seventies.

■ **KAFFEERÖSTEREI RUBENS**
Emmastrasse 7 (Rüttenscheid)
▲ Martinstrasse
◆ Tue-Fri 10am-2pm + 3-6pm, Sat 10am-2pm

You can buy coffee just about everywhere, but rarely in such a lovely setting. What's more, the beans are roasted on the premises!

■ **KÖSTERS AM THEATER**
I. Hagen 26 (city centre)
▲ Hirschlandplatz
◆ Mon-Fri 10am-6.30pm, Sat 10am-6pm

Classic design items, out-of-the-ordinary kitchen ware or high-class table ware: it's all here on three floors packed with unusual ideas for gifts.

Kaffeerösterei Rubens

■ **KINDERPARADIES ESSEN**
Frankenstrasse 274
(Stadtwald)
▲ Stadtwald
◆ Mon-Tue, Thu-Fri 9.30am-6pm, Wed+Sat 9.30am-2pm

Everything for kids can be found here.

■ **PROUST WÖRTER + TÖNE**
Akazienallee/Am Handelshof 1 (city centre)
▲ Hauptbahnhof
◆ Mon-Fri 10am-8pm
Sat 10am-4pm

A small but high-class bookshop, which presents not only the offerings of the major publishing houses in the field of literature but also gems from small independent publishers.

■ **TWENTYNINE PALMS**
Bertoldstrasse 4
(Rüttenscheid)
▲ Rüttenscheider Stern
◆ Mon-Fri 11am-8.30pm,
Sat 11am-3pm

A concept store for home items and accessories in Scandinavian style, straightforward and functional with clear design reduced to essentials.

■ **WOHNGEMEINSCHAFT**
Hedwigstrasse 7
(south quater)
▲ Rüttenscheider Stern
◆ Mon-Fri 11am-7pm,
Sat 10am-3pm

If you want to go browsing away from the main shopping streets, here you will find high-quality design products – from postcards and clothing to sofas – made by creative local people.

KulturLinie 107
See and experience the transformation of Essen from an industrial to a service city: you can do this with KulturLinie 107, operated by the local transport authority, Essener Verkehrs-AG (EVAG). It runs from the green south of Essen to Gelsenkirchen via the main station and Zeche Zollverein on a 17-kilometre route connecting 60 cultural sights, including two major museums, two opera houses, the cathedral, the Philharmonie and the World Heritage cultural site of Zeche Zollverein. With the help of KulturLinie 107, visitors can be guided conveniently through the city and find their way thanks to the signs at the individual stops. You can now also take line no. 108, but at the Essen main station you have to change to line no. 107.

www.kulturlinie107.de

Addresses

Service

University
The University Duisburg-Essen lies on the edge of the city centre. With around 40,000 students enrolled and 4,500 employees it is one of the largest in Germany. It is also one of the youngest as well, having being created in 2003 out of the merger of the universities in Duisburg and Essen. Practically everything can be studied here, whereby the spectrum extends from well-developed courses in the humanities, social sciences and economics over the highly respected design courses to engineering, the natural sciences and medicine. Right next door a high-class quarter for living, working and leisure with extensive areas of water and park, promenades and several squares is being created: "Universitätsviertel – grüne mitte Essen" is the name of this leafy and central district.

www.uni-due.de
www.gruene-mitte-essen.de

60

■ INFORMATION
EMG Essen Marketing GmbH
Touristikzentrale
Am Hauptbahnhof 2 (city)
45127 Essen
Tel. 0201/8872041
Fax: 0201/8872018
◆ Mon-Fri 9am-5pm,
Sat 10am-1pm
www.essen-marketing.de

■ BANKS
The banks in the city centre are open during the usual business hours (approx. 8.30am-4pm).
Reisebank
(in the central railway station)
◆ Mon-Sat 7.30am-7.30pm, Sun 9.30am-1pm

■ GERMAN RAILWAYS
Tel. 0180/6996633
www.bahn.de

■ ADVANCE TICKET BOOKING
NRW Tickets Limited
Frankenstrasse 256,
Tel. 0201/4378571
TicketCenter,
II. Hagen 2,
Tel. 0201/8122200
WAZ/NRZ-LeserLaden
Kornmarkt 4 (city centre)
Tel. 0800/6060716

■ Media
Papers: Neue Ruhr/Rhein Zeitung (NRZ), taz ruhr, Westdeutsche Allgemeine (WAZ), Radio: Neue Essener Welle, Radio Essen, Ruhr Rock Radio, WDR Studio Essen

■ CAR RENTALS
Avis 01806/217702
Europcar 040/520188000
Hertz 01806/333535
Sixt 01806/252525

■ EMERGENCY MEDICAL CARE ON-DUTY MEDICAL UNIT
Tel. 01805/044100,
PHARMACY SERVICE
www.aponet.de

■ PUBLIC TRANSPORT
Essener Verkehrs AG (EVAG)
www.evag.de
Timetable and price info
Tel. 0201/8261234
Customer care at the main rail station
◆ Mon-Fri 8am-6pm,
Sat 9am-2pm (May)

■ CENTRAL POST OFFICE
Willy-Brandt-Platz 1
◆ Mon-Fri 8am-7pm,
Sat 9.30am-3.30pm

■ ESSEN WELCOMECARD
For an individual or a group, for one, two or three days, with the ESSEN.WELCOMECARD. you can travel free of charge on public transport in the city of Essen and get discounts and free services in restaurants and bars, as well as for boat trips on the Baldeneysee and bike hire. The ESSEN.WELCOMECARD can

be purchased from the two customer centres, 80 partners, some 210 ticket machines of the transport authority EVAG and from the EMG tourist office.

■ SIGHTSEEING TOURS GUIDED TOUR TAXI
"Tour de Essen" – up to seven people in a large taxi.
Tel. 0201/666066

REGIONALVERBAND RUHRGEBIET (RVR) RUHRTOUR
Kronprinzenstrasse 35, 45128 Essen
Tel. 0201/20690
www.rvr-online.de
DIE REVIERPROFIS
Tel. 0208/8470349
www.revierprofis.de
CITY EXCURSION
www.essener-stadtrundfahrten.de
Tour de Ruhr
Emscherstrasse 71, 47137 Duisburg
Tel. 0203/4291919
www.tour-de-ruhr.de
ZEITSPRUNG
Kokerei Zollverein, Tor 3,
Tel. 0201/28958-0
www.zeitsprung-agentur.de

■ TAXI CALL
Tel. 0201/19410 + 86655

Taxi companies in Essen drive the environmentally friendly UTE taxis than run on natural gas (with the support of the public utility company Stadtwerke AG).

■ WEBSITES
www.essen.de
www.ruhr-guide.de
www.messe-essen.de
www.ewg.de

■ IMPORTANT ADDRESSES
CONGRESS CENTER ESSEN GMBH
Norbertstrasse, 45131 Essen
Tel. 0201/7244878
www.cc-essen.de
ESSEN MARKETING GMBH
Rathenaustrasse 2
45127 Essen
Tel. 0201/887200
www.essen-marketing.de
EWG ESSENER WIRTSCHAFTSFÖR-DERUNGSGESELLSCHAFT MBH
Lindenallee 55
45127 Essen
Tel. 0201/820240
www.ewg.de
INDUSTRIE- UND HANDELSKAMMER (IHK)
Am Waldthausenpark 2
45127 Essen
Tel. 0201/18920
www.essen.ihk24.de
MESSE ESSEN GMBH
Norbertstrasse
45131 Essen
Tel. 0201/72440
www.messe-essen.de

Essen – a green city
Anyone who thinks Essen is still a place of coal mines and smoking factory chimneys could hardly be more wrong. Essen's many parks, nature reserves, woods, lakes and other open spaces account for almost half of the area within the city boundaries, which makes Essen the greenest city in North Rhine-Westphalia according to official statistics. Essen has more than 2300 hectares of recreational areas, over 2800 hectares of woodland and almost 600 hectares of water – the equivalent of some 8000 football pitches of nothing but nature. It is estimated that three million trees grow in the city. More than 40 municipal parks and gardens provide leisure facilities and places to relax.

Essen's historical dates

ca. 800	Liudger, missionary and first Bishop of Münster, founds a Benedictine abbey in what is today the Werden district.
852	Altfrid, Bishop of Hildesheim, founds a convent for the daughters of the high nobility.
946	The collegiate church is reconstructed after a fire.
971 to 1011	Abbess Mathilde II enriches the church treasures during her term of office with valuable pieces like the Golden Madonna.
1039 to 1058	Abbess Theophanu adds the West nave to the Ottonian church.
1041	King Henry II grants the convent settlement market rights.
1216	Emperor Frederick II designates the abbess as "Princess of the Realm".
1244	Essen receives its town charter. The princess-abbess is de facto deprived of her power, which led to constant conflicts until 1803.
1275	Albert the Great consecrates the rebuilt abbey church.
1317	The existence of coal in the Essen region is mentioned for the first time.
1377	Charles IV grants the town the title "Free City of the Realm".
1563	The town council introduces the Reformation in Essen.
1620	The Essen forge already produces 14,000 rifles and pistols.
1802	Prussian troops occupy Essen.
1803	The Cathedral Chapter of Essen and Werden Abbey are secularised in the wake of the decision to abolish all religious principalities.
1809	With the first conveyor steam engine, Franz Dinnendahl creates the most important precondition for deep-cast coal mining.

1826	The 14-year-old Alfred Krupp takes over the 1811 founded cast steel works from his father.
1852	Alfred Krupp's seamless rail wheel flange makes his company the largest in the 19th century.
1896	Essen becomes a major city with a total of more than 100,000 inhabitants.
1906	Margarethe Krupp donates the Margarethenhöhe residential estate on the marriage of her daughter Bertha to Gustav von Bohlen und Halbach.
1932	Shaft XII of the Zollverein colliery starts operations.
1938	The synagogue and other Jewish buildings are destroyed during the "Night of Broken Glass" state pogrom.
1945	As the result of air raids during World War II, 90 percent of the city centre has been destroyed.
1946 to 1949	Gustav Heinemann – later President of Germany – is Lord Mayor of Essen.
1958 to 1973	Almost all mines cease coal production during the mining industry crisis.
1965	The Federal Garden Show takes place in the Gruga Park.
1972	The University of Essen opens its gates to students for the first time.
1986	The Zollverein – the last Essen coalmine still in production – is shut down.
2001	The Zollverein colliery and coking plant become part of the UNESCO World Cultural Heritage.
2002	Essen celebrates its 1,150-year jubilee.
2006	Essen is chosen as European Capital of Culture 2010 on behalf of the Ruhr area.
2010	Opening of the Ruhr Museum.
2011	Krupp celebrates 200-years history of the company.
2017	Essen is the European Green Capital.

Register

Picture Credits

All photos BKB Verlag except Aalto Musiktheater/Foti Gerd Weigelt U1 be.r.; Abraham Konditorei & Café Werntges 25 be.l.; Affentheater 48 ab.; Altkatholische Friedenskirche 15 Mi.l.; Attila Csörgö 57 ab.; Baliha Dance Club 49 ab.r.; Casino Zollverein GmbH 35 be.l.; Congress Center Essen GmbH 52 ab.; Design Zentrum Nordrhein Westfalen 32 ab.r., 35 Mi.; Dinnebier Licht GmbH 11 ab.r.; Domschatzkammer Essen 18 ab.l., be.r.; Domschatzkammer Essen © Anne Gold 17 Mi.; Esszimmer 44 be., 45 Mi.l.; Equitana 42 ab., Essen Intercity Hotel 44 r.; Essen Sheraton Hotel 11 ab.l.; 40 Mi.; Folkwang Hochschule 24 ab.l.; Folkwang Hochschule © Georg Schreiber 24 Mi.l.; Hans Peter Hüster & Frank Mohn © ART & WEISE FILM 12 ab.r.; Hotel „An der Gruga" 38 r.; Hotel Maximilians 39 ab.l.; Hubert Imhoff GmbH 41 be.; Idko GmbH 43 be.; Jochen Tack/Stiftung Zollverein U8; Kaffeerösterei Rubens 58 be.; Kulturstiftung Ruhr 22 ab.r., 23 Mi.l.; Kulturzentrum Schloss Borbeck/Peter Wieler 41 Mi.; Kunsthaus Essen 56 be.; Margarethe Krupp Stiftung für Wohnungsfürsorge 23 ab.l., Mi.r., 62 ab.l.; Markt- und Schaustellermuseum 57 be.; Martin Engelbrecht 16 ab., 17 ab.r., 18 Mi., 19 Mi., be.; Maze 48 be.; Mc Donald's Kinderhilfe Stiftung 51 ab.; Messe Essen GmbH 39 be., 49 be.; Messe Essen GmbH/Rainer Schimm 38 l.; Mintrops Land Hotel Burgaltendorf 40 be., Museum Folkwang 30; Museum Folkwang/NMFE GmbH 31 ab.r.; Pact Zollverein/Thomas Mayer 35 ab.r.; Peter Wieler/ Essen Marketing: U 1 ab., 2–3, 10–11 be., 12 be., 14 Mi.r., be., 15 ab.r., 22 ab.l., 25 be.r., 32 be., 33 Mi., 34 Mi., 35 ab.l., 37 ab.r., 40 ab.l., 51 Mi., 54 ab., 58 r.; Peter Zingel 27 Mi.r.; Philharmonie Essen © PE / Sven Lorenz 5, Ruhr 2010/Manfred Vollmer 37 Mi., be.; Ruhr 2010/Matthias Duschner 52 be.; Ruhrmuseum 34 ab.l.; Ruhrtriennale©Helge Thelen 53 ab. , 56 ab.; Ruhr-tourismus/Stefan Ziese 50 be.; Ruhrtriennale©Pascal Victor 55; RWE AG 1, 11 Mi.r., 31 Mi.; Schauspiel Essen/Foto Thilo Ben 54 be.; Schloss Hugenpoet 40–41 ab.; Seaside Beach Baldeney 50 Mi.l.; Seaside Beach Baldeney 47 ab.; Spielstättenfoto Reinhart Cosaert© Ministerium für Dezember 2002 18 be.l.; Stadtbildstelle Essen 23 be.; Stadt Essen/Peter Prengel U1 u.l.; Stage Entertainment 53 be.; Stiftung Zollverein 4 ab., 33 ab.r.; Stratmanns Theater 13 be.r.; Table Service Team 11 Mi.l.; Theater und Philharmonie Essen GmbH/Michael Kneffel 10 ab.r.; ThyssenKrupp AG 14 Mi.l., 22 Mi., 35 be.r., 63; Universität Duisburg-Essen 60ab.; Zollverein School of Management and Design 34 Mi.